APPLICATION DEVELOPMENT FOR THE 90s

Computer Associates Application Development Strategy For Mainframe, Midrange, Network and PC Environments

Printed in the United States of America.

ISBN 0-923108-09-2

CONTENTS

Section I

Development Challenges And The CA Solutions

Section II

Planning, Management And Design

Section III

Legacy Systems

Section IV

Applications For The New Environments

PREFACE

Application developers face intriguing challenges in the new computing environments of the 90s. Mainframe, midrange and desktop systems combined in a myriad of configurations present new possibilities as they create new problems. Developers are expected to combine the throughput, reliability, integrity and security that the mainframe world achieved after 30 years with the economy, convenience, flexibility and elegance to which the desktop world only recently aspired.

Beyond these purely technical considerations, business pressures loom large. The competitive and cost-conscious business world requires vigorous exploitation of new technologies. The evolution to decentralized business practices requires a corresponding evolution to distributed processing.

This changing landscape of business and technology has far-reaching impact on application development. Developers must learn and integrate a number of new technologies, without "dropping the ball" that keeps business running.

Faced with these challenges, developers should consider that in some languages, the word for "crisis" is a combination of the words for "danger" and "opportunity." By exploiting the opportunity for revolutionary advances while watching out for the danger of losing existing assets, developers can turn this crisis into an occasion for greatness. If new technology can be combined with old, the technical elegance of the new ideas can be turned into a real-world business benefit.

Computer Associates presents an application development strategy that successfully marries the old with the new. It provides the wealth of integrated development tools needed to enable the fast development of powerful, modern applications for the new computing environments. At the same time, it provides the means to protect and leverage investments in existing systems.

This unique application development strategy is supported by and acts as the delivery vehicle for *CA90s: Computing Architecture For The 90s*, the blueprint for the development of all CA software.

Application Development For The 90s describes Computer Associates strategy and the Application Development Software derived from it. The strategy effectively guides enterprises through the tumultuous, confusing plethora of paths available to application developers. It provides a comprehensive plan for moving to the new computing environments of the future. Even more importantly, it is based on software solutions that exist today and that possess the flexibility to incorporate the emerging trends of tomorrow.

The book is divided into four sections:

I. *Development Challenges And The CA Solutions*

A discussion of the challenges facing developers and the technical and business pressures behind them, followed by an overview of the CA solutions, of CA90s from the perspective of application development, and the open database architecture that forms a foundation for the development systems.

II. *Planning, Management And Design*

A description of the support facilities necessary for the management of the development process itself, including analysis and design, iterative development, schedule and resource management, and life cycle management. These facilities apply across the board, regardless of what kind of application is being built and what platform is used.

III. *Legacy Systems*

A description of those tools and facilities that support maintenance and enhancement of legacy systems, those applications built on traditional platforms that form the foundation for most current business processing. These facilities include support for offloading development to workstations and downsizing applications to midrange and desktop platforms.

IV. *Applications For The New Environments*

A description of the development systems aimed at exploiting the new technologies, including object-oriented systems, visual development tools, graphical user interfaces and client/server architectures. These systems are designed to leverage existing expertise and applications by integrating new technologies with traditional systems and languages.

Note that this book is not intended to provide detailed commitments for specific product releases, features and delivery dates. Rather it is a description of the strategy and principles, supported by CA90s and specific CA products, that clients as well as CA staff can follow in order to conquer the challenges facing application development today and in the future.

ACKNOWLEDGMENTS

Computer Associates strategy for application development across mainframe, midrange and desktop systems is based on the input received from thousands of CA clients worldwide. We want to extend our thanks to our clients who continue to guide us by communicating their needs so clearly.

In addition, we would like to recognize the tremendous contributions made by CA employees in defining and expressing the strategy for application development as well as in utilizing the strategy to engineer superior CA software solutions. A special thanks is owed to Russ Artzt, Nancy Li, Dominique Laborde, the Product Owners and the developers who so patiently and painstakingly clarified technical product details and strategies for us.

Anders Vinberg deserves special mention for not only helping to shape Computer Associates application development strategy, but for being the primary author of and the driving force behind this book. Our thanks extend as well to Beth Bloom, Christine Spinosa and the talented members of Computer Associates Creative departments for their invaluable assistance in writing, editing, designing and producing this book.

Finally, we would like to acknowledge our families who showed a great deal of understanding during long days, nights and weekends.

SECTION I

Development Challenges And The CA Solutions

CHAPTER 1

The Application Development Challenges

Application development is in the midst of a revolutionary restructuring. Within just five years, the shape of application development will be so different that it will seem unrecognizable to a 1980s developer. The driving force behind these changes is the desire to take advantage of new technologies that promise to lower the costs and improve the performance of applications, make them easier to learn and use, and improve the productivity and quality of the development process itself. Yet, as these changes take hold, reality—limited budgets and the legacy of existing applications—demands that the new applications coexist with the systems that millions of business people depend on every day.

The challenge is to combine the new with the old: to exploit graphical user interfaces, object orientation, heterogeneous computing environments, client/server architectures and distributed processing while maintaining and enhancing hundreds of strategic "legacy" applications. How can developers learn all these new techniques, master the new tools and restructure their business solutions without losing the momentum that keeps business running? This is the challenge we address in this book.

Building these new systems would be a difficult challenge even without the issue of legacy systems. When targeting the new computing environment as a platform for mission-critical line-of-business applications, we expect it to meet the highest standards of performance, reliability, availability, integrity and security—standards that the traditional mainframe environment achieved after 30 years. At the same time, we expect dramatic improvement in usability, flexibility and elegance to levels that personal desktop solutions only recently achieved.

And even without these technical challenges, the development process needs strengthening to meet the demands of today's fast-moving business environment. Development productivity is still lower than it should be, backlogs are longer than they should be and applications are less flexible than they need to be. Developers need new tools and techniques that can deal effectively with rapidly evolving requirements and make IS an effective partner in a competitive business world.

We are surrounded by new, "revolutionary" technologies that claim to address all these problems. But the extravagant claims and lack of demonstrable success of the advocates of new technologies and development methodologies only deepens the skepticism of experienced developers.

But discarding the new technologies would be as wrong as abandoning the old. The potential benefits of graphical user interfaces, client/server architectures and object-oriented development are very real and very pragmatic. The right way to deal with the dilemma is to find ways to use the new technologies to leverage investments in existing systems.

The New Computing Environment

Most industry observers agree that the computing environment of the future is a "heterogeneous client/server LAN": a local area network with relatively low-cost client workstations with graphical user interfaces, high-powered servers, a mix of systems of different brand names and operating systems, and connectivity to other networks and mainframes. Today, the client workstations are most likely Intel-based PCs running under DOS or increasingly Windows, OS/2 or NT. A RISC-based machine or a high-end, multi-processor Intel-based machine running UNIX, OS/2 or NT holds the greatest promise as the server. The most common configuration today is still homogeneous, from all-DOS to all-UNIX, but most development managers must be prepared to deal with heterogeneous environments during this decade.

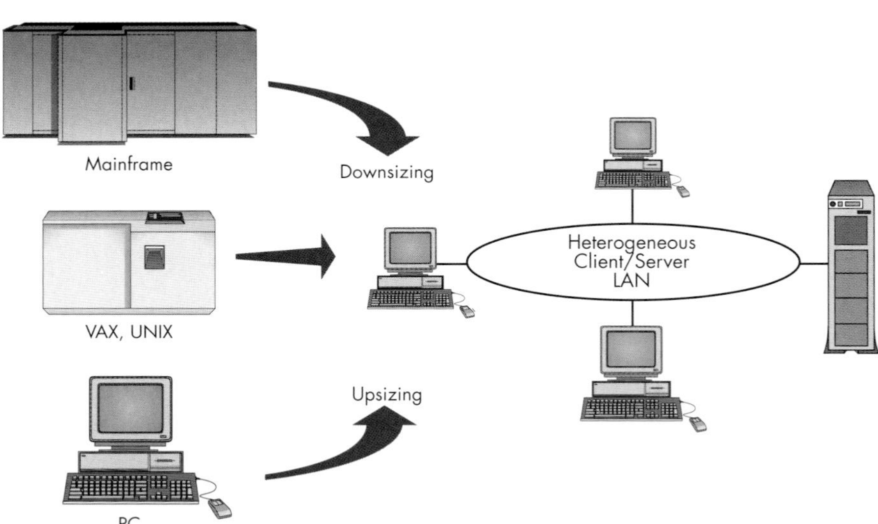

The "environment of the future," a heterogeneous Local Area Network with client/server application architectures, is the migration target for IS users from all environments.

IS users congregate on this new environment from three different directions:

- **Downsizing of mainframe solutions**—this requires a robust platform to meet the performance and integrity demands of mission-critical applications.
- **UNIX and VAX solutions**—these often use networks with client/server application architectures; in the new world, the networks increasingly include PCs.
- **Upsizing of PC solutions**—successful solutions built for individuals, small groups or departments grow to address larger user groups, data volumes and transaction rates.

As the desktop computer gains more and more power, new demands are placed on it by new kinds of applications. A desktop machine with dozens of megabytes of memory, dozens of MIPS, hundreds of megabytes of disk and network connections is no longer a "personal computer." It is a small, inexpensive mainframe, and many users expect to make the same demands on its applications as on larger systems.

In this transition to the client/server LAN environment, the three groups with their very different backgrounds have the same concerns and, to their great surprise, find they can learn from one another. They are facing an unprecedented challenge: building mission-critical line-of-business applications with the security, integrity, reliability and throughput of a mainframe, ease of use and convenience of a PC, and power, economy and flexibility of a UNIX system. The solutions require the best from all worlds.

Strengths And Weaknesses Of PC Computing

Over the last decade, PCs have come to dominate many areas of computing—not just personal productivity, but increasingly business processing as well. This success comes largely from the software development techniques used, not just the low cost of equipment. PC applications are commonly built with high-level, high-productivity tools that support iterative development methods and incremental refinement. And one of the most important factors is not technology, but attitude—the philosophy of prioritizing ergonomics above most other considerations.

A desktop machine with dozens of megabytes of memory, dozens of MIPS, hundreds of megabytes of disk and network connections is no longer a "personal computer," it is a small mainframe.

The Graphical User Interface (GUI) is of particular importance. These environments—Windows, PM, Motif and the Macintosh—provide an important foundation for applications beyond just the cosmetics and convenience of mouse, menus and graphics. With support for multitasking and built-in facilities for intertask communication such as the clipboard, DDE and OLE, Windows and its siblings are in some ways more powerful than larger systems. Applications need to exploit these environments fully.

Two weaknesses of PC computing make it difficult to extend its success to line-of-business applications. The technical foundation of languages and databases like dBASE, the most commonly used system for business programming in the PC world, cannot be readily scaled up to the demands of larger systems. And the development methods often lack the rigor necessary to support larger development teams and ensure the integrity of mission-critical applications. The evolution of PCs into full-fledged members of enterprise computing requires combining the flexibility and elegance of the PC with the robustness and rigor of traditional IS.

Legacy Systems

The so-called "legacy systems," the existing applications that provide the foundation for running business today, pose a dilemma. Migrating these applications to new environments, new architectures and new user interfaces is a formidable task. Yet, legacy systems constitute the major asset of IS. Rebuilding from scratch what took 30 years to build is not only impractical and uneconomical, it is physically impossible.

We must find ways to reengineer these legacy systems, restructuring them to suit the new environments and new architectures. This might involve modification of individual programs to utilize new technologies, or restructuring the overall system by "surrounding" mainframe programs with graphical workstations. Such heterogeneous distributed processing holds great promise, but is of course quite demanding from an engineering viewpoint.

Rebuilding from scratch what took 30 years to build is not only impractical and uneconomical, it is physically impossible.

dBASE Legacy Systems

Most analysts take the term "legacy systems" to mean mainframe, COBOL, 3270 applications only. Yet, many CA clients report that their investment in Xbase (dBASE, CA-Clipper, FoxPro) applications is as large as their mainframe investment. The implications of converting Xbase and similar applications to graphical user interfaces and client/server architectures are just as challenging as for mainframe applications—indeed, often more so since development practices were less rigorous and there is often less documentation on the PC applications. Protecting and leveraging investments in these "second-generation legacy systems" and moving the applications to the modern world is another major challenge.

Downsizing

The term "downsizing" is used to describe a number of different strategies. To set priorities and select tools and techniques for downsizing, these strategies must be analyzed separately and their objectives explicitly stated. CA clients have described three separate steps to exploiting desktop and midrange systems:

1. *Offloading Development And Maintenance*

   Reducing costs and improving productivity by offloading to desktop workstations the development and maintenance of applications intended for execution on mainframes.

   Key requirements: a complete development environment, control and management of the distributed development process, support for test execution, and 100 percent compatibility with the mainframe production environment.

2. *Downsizing Production Execution*

   Saving money, improving operational flexibility or distributing business processing by moving production execution to lower cost platforms.

   Key requirements: 100 percent compatibility with mainframe, plus performance, reliability, security and integrity during execution.

3. *Exploiting The New Platforms And Technologies*

   Improving ergonomics and increasing flexibility with graphical user interfaces, integration with personal productivity software, and support for unstructured data and quality printing.

   Key requirements: platform exploitation, performance, reliability, integrity. Mainframe compatibility is beneficial, but 100 percent compatibility is not required, since the applications will by definition be changed to exploit new technologies.

The different objectives of the downsizing strategies require different technical solutions. For example, when the objective is cost reduction, major reengineering is not practical—existing applications must be recycled and leveraged. Graphical tools help improve development productivity, but making the applications themselves graphical is a usability and not a cost reduction move. Once the objectives of the strategy are made explicit, a suitable enabling technology can be chosen.

The different objectives of the downsizing strategies require different technical solutions.

Development And Maintenance Of Mainframe Applications

Studies have shown that a consistently short response time significantly improves both productivity and quality of software development and maintenance. A desktop workstation can provide the mainframe programmer with a very powerful and cost-effective environment. Programming, compilation and testing on a workstation not only lowers cost and improves productivity, it also reduces the risk of development and maintenance impacting production systems.

The challenge lies in exploiting modern workstation technology in the development and maintenance of applications intended for mainframe execution. The developer needs an integrated, distributed development environment that combines graphical programming, analysis and debugging tools with mainframe compilation and testing, and networked life cycle management. This can combine a consistent graphical workbench for both mainframe- and desktop-based development with the security and integrity protection of established mainframe systems.

New Development Methods For A New World

The business world of the 90s moves fast. Technology moves fast. The only certainty is change. In this world, application development must be light on its feet.

The traditional development life cycle with its linear flow is based on the idea of producing a "final product" based on original design specifications. Regardless of the merit of techniques for improving the productivity and accuracy of the steps in this procedure, there is increasing recognition that this very idea is incapable of handling the world of today and tomorrow. Business needs evolve too quickly to allow the specifications of the "final product" to last very long. Recognizing that change is a natural part of life, we need a development model that can accommodate continual change.

Most of the traditional approaches to improving development speed and productivity do not cope well with the pressures of this rapidly evolving world. One that remains effective is code reuse. Indeed, code reuse is perhaps the only economy of scale available in software engineering.

Code reuse can also improve application reliability. Regardless of what development methodology is used, no newly written program is as reliable as one that has been thoroughly tested in practice. It is sobering to consider that FAA reliability regulations for aircraft control equipment explicitly exclude software because its reliability cannot be measured or even predicted—in their words, "it is not feasible to assess the number or kinds of software errors that may remain after the completion of system design, development and test." Development methodologies must aid in the creation of better software, not just speed up the development process.

Code reuse is perhaps the only economy of scale available in software engineering.

Producing complete and correct specifications to feed the process is increasingly difficult as the time scale of the cycle shortens. Because one of the main sources of "errors" in software is incorrect or out-of-date requirements specifications, techniques such as prototyping that are aimed at improving the definition process can have a direct impact on the quality of the solution, not just the productivity of the process.

These trends in business and technology have led to an increasing interest in an *iterative development process.* Successful development tools must support this process and facilitate code reuse. Technologies such as visual development, object orientation and integrated repositories effectively enable this paradigm.

Reengineering For New Technologies

The new technologies in desktop and network environments have significant implications for application development. The greatest challenges come from graphical user interfaces and distributed application architectures including client/server structures.

Graphical user interface programming is extremely complex, primarily because of the flexible, event-driven nature of a GUI application. Rather than the program controlling the sequence of events, the end user can request any action at any time. Indeed, a well-designed GUI program should be prepared to redisplay its screen at any time, with a delay of no more than one tenth of a second, even in the middle of some major processing task. The requirement for screen refresh may be caused by actions of other programs, so logical analysis of program flow is not relevant. Similarly, a program may be interrupted in the middle of a large I/O or processing task, and it should not only suspend the operation and respond immediately to the interruption, but must also determine whether the operator action invalidated the operation, and either continue or abandon it. This is a radical shift from the traditional programming paradigm, one that goes far beyond the mere cosmetics of the GUI environment.

Exploiting these technologies requires partial restructuring of applications. Adapting existing programs to the event-driven structure of GUI applications and partitioning process logic to fit the client/server architecture require disassembling them and reassembling their business logic in new ways. This "recycling" of applications requires compatible development systems that support standard languages in the new structures. It also requires analysis tools that visualize the structure of complex programs to help the developer identify separate program segments that can be made to fit the new architectures.

Object Orientation, Visual Development And Repository-Based Environments

New technologies such as object orientation and visual development systems can significantly improve development productivity. The demands of GUI programming fueled its acceptance, but object orientation is an effective tool for managing complexity in general—and complexity is at the root of most IS challenges. The technology is gradually entering the mainstream of business programming, initially for new development of limited departmental applications. Over time, mainstream-oriented tools and training will allow its use in mission-critical line-of-business systems.

GUI programming fueled its acceptance, but object orientation is an effective tool for managing complexity in general.

Visual development is well suited to rapid development, prototyping and joint end-user design—the key techniques for meeting the needs of today's fast-moving business world. Combined with a code generator, visual development is an effective tool for development of all applications, including mission-critical ones.

Realizing the full benefits of these technologies requires a different approach to development. A development environment closely integrated with an online repository can provide significantly improved development productivity. It also helps ensure the integrity of the application, by not only enabling code reuse, but by making it convenient and promoting consistent use of code and data.

Distributed Processing And Client/Server Architectures

Many developers find that the most practical approach to adopting the new technologies is often a combination of legacy systems and new applications. Database server solutions allow GUI-based workstations to directly access the host system databases that the legacy systems use. But in many cases, this is not enough. Application-level distribution is required to "surround" existing applications with GUI-based workstations. New enabling technologies must support application-level distributed processing between workstations and legacy systems. The client/server architectures must support database servers as well as application servers.

Investment Protection And Leverage

Like all development tools, these new technologies must fit within established languages and architectures. History tells us that this is essential because of the fundamental obligation of IS to protect and leverage existing investments. As long as object orientation was available only in new, unknown languages, for example, it could not expand beyond its academic niche. A move to graphical user interfacing and object orientation will always require training in new concepts and new design and development techniques; it should not require training in new languages.

The investment in applications is a major asset of most IS organizations—but the most important asset is the people who built them, the expertise of the developers who know the business problems and their solutions. New technologies must leverage these assets, people and programs alike.

CHAPTER 2

CA Application Development Solutions

CA Application Development Software is designed to meet new and old challenges facing IS development. By combining modern tools and techniques with a commitment to optimizing client investments in legacy systems, CA Application Development Software helps developers quickly and effectively build new applications that take advantage of new technology. In addition, CA Application Development Software eases the migration of legacy applications from mainframe to midrange and desktop systems, and enables the enhancement of legacy applications to benefit from new technology.

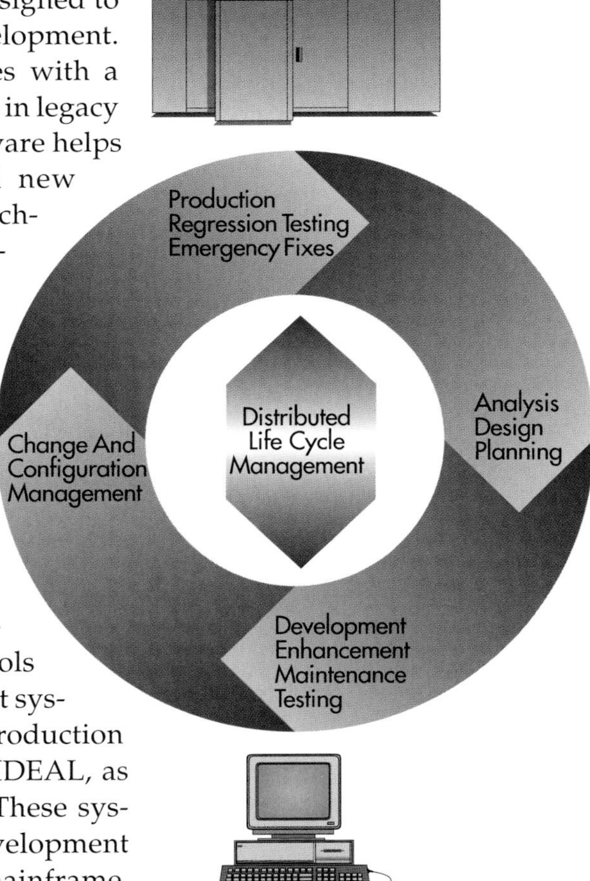

A distributed maintenance and development environment for legacy applications integrates mainframes, networks and workstations.

Legacy Systems

To help mainframe developers take advantage of the power and responsiveness of desktop workstations, CA Application Development Software provides languages and tools for offloading development. The development systems most commonly used in mainframe production applications are COBOL, CA-ADS and CA-IDEAL, as well as CA-EASYTRIEVE and CA-RAMIS. These systems are all available in the form of PC development workstations, fully compatible with the mainframe. These PC versions support offloading development, as well as downsizing production execution to PC and network environments. For downsizing to midrange systems, the development systems and databases are also available on VAX/VMS and UNIX systems. These development systems support client/server architectures, both database servers and application-level distributed processing.

CA-TELON is the major application generator used to produce COBOL and PL/I code. The CA-TELON PWS development workstation operates under DOS and OS/2 and generates code for mainframes, AS/400, UNIX, Tandem, OS/2 and DOS systems.

For offloading development and maintenance of mainframe legacy applications, the CA-Realia II distributed development environment provides a graphical, Windows-based workstation that connects networks, midrange systems and mainframes. It integrates the graphical analysis and debugging facilities of CA-COBOLVISION with facilities for development and building of COBOL programs, as well as distributed library management and change control.

On PCs, the legacy role is played by the Xbase family of languages: dBASE, CA-Clipper, CA-dBFast and FoxPro. CA-Clipper is extended with support for client/server architectures and object orientation under DOS; through CA-Clipper/Compiler Kit For dBASE IV, the same facilities are provided for dBASE.

Exploiting New Technologies

For development of new applications that exploit the new computing environment, under Windows, OS/2, NT or Motif, the CA-Visual Objects system provides a suite of powerful new technologies. It adds support for iterative development with a graphical user interface, visual development tools and a repository-based integrated development environment. These technologies are based on a strong foundation of object-oriented, industrial-strength compiler and client/server technologies.

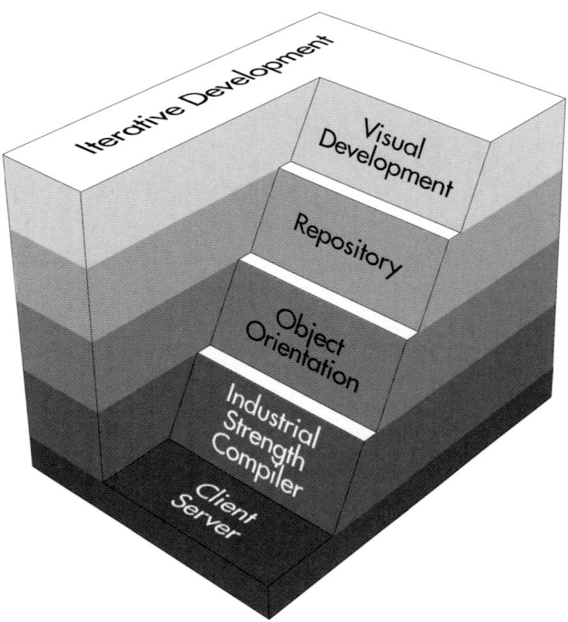

High-level visual tools for iterative development are built on a solid bedrock of a repository-based framework, object orientation, industrial-strength compiler technology and client/server architectures.

CA-Visual Objects forms the basis for extending all the mainstream business languages: CA-Clipper, CA-dBFast, dBASE, FoxPro, COBOL, CA-ADS, CA-IDEAL and CA-TELON. This combination of new technology and language familiarity protects and leverages investments in existing technologies, and, perhaps more importantly, protects and leverages current expertise. It also fulfills the potential of the new technologies, finally allowing object orientation, for example, to benefit real-world commercial programming. While object orientation and GUI technology bring COBOL, CA-ADS and CA-IDEAL into the world of the new computing environments, the industrial-strength compiler and client/server facilities bring the Xbase languages into the world of mission-critical applications, with the same kind of integrity and performance as C and COBOL.

CA-Visual Objects (based on the well-known "Aspen" research project) is based on five key technologies designed to make the migration from old to new worlds effective and efficient:

- **Open architecture**—ensuring that applications can access all industry standard databases, support any established language, utilize components built with other languages and development systems, and include new tools created by third parties
- **Hybrid technology**—ensuring that applications can combine the performance and integrity of compiled languages and database access with the flexibility and responsiveness of interpreted, dynamic systems, and enabling the "wrapping" of legacy code within the structure of an object-oriented, GUI-based application
- **Visual technology**—providing visual development tools for all aspects of the system to improve productivity and lower the barriers to building the sophisticated applications of the future
- **Incremental technology**—providing integral support for the iterative development process, prototyping and reuse of code
- **Industrial-strength technology**—ensuring that the end result is robust enough to meet the ever-increasing demands of business and that the development process has the rigor and integrity to form the foundation of business development

For technical and system programming where the C and C++ languages dominate, the CA-C++ platform-independent compiler and the CA-CommonView platform-adaptive GUI class library for C++ provide a robust, multi-platform foundation.

Planning, Management And Design

The management of the development process is as important as the purely technical aspects. Projects must be estimated, planned and budgeted. System requirements must be analyzed and solutions designed. Schedules, deliverables and resources must be tracked and managed. Results must be measured and reported. The applications themselves must be controlled, secured, distributed and released.

CA development management tools provide comprehensive life cycle management for the distributed development environment. Workstations are automatically integrated with production mainframe libraries. Analysis and design tools ("front-end CASE") are automatically integrated with implementation systems.

Language Strategy

The CA Application Development Software strategy includes support for each of the commonly used languages. While these languages have different characteristics, they have in common the fact that developers know them well and know how to use them effectively. As the industry undergoes revolutionary changes, CA strategy is based on preserving developers' expertise by integrating new technologies with existing languages. Major new technologies such as visual development and the object-oriented framework are shared among the different language products and present a common philosophy, but each language preserves its unique flavor to ensure that the developer sees a familiar world.

Product	Legacy Environments	New Technologies
CA-Clipper	DOS version gains extended object orientation and client/server support	Migration path to GUI environments is provided by CA-Visual Objects for Clipper, with full object orientation, visual development tools, repository-based development environment and client/server support
CA-dBFast		Grows into the CA-Visual Objects architecture, initially with extended visual development tools and later with full object orientation
dBASE, FoxPro	CA-Clipper/Compiler Kit For dBASE IV provides higher performance for dBASE applications under DOS	Follow the same growth path as the CA Xbase languages, with CA-Visual Objects versions that combine language and database compatibility with full support for object orientation, GUI, visual development and client/server technology
COBOL	CA-Realia on PCs, suitable both for offloading development and downsizing production systems; a distributed, visual workbench streamlines the entire development and maintenance process	CA-Visual Objects for COBOL provides migration path to new technologies
CA-ADS	Available on PC-LAN, VAX/VMS and UNIX systems, together with CA-IDMS	CA-Visual Objects for ADS provides migration path to new technologies
CA-IDEAL	Available on PC-LAN, VAX/VMS and UNIX systems, together with CA-DATACOM	CA-Visual Objects for IDEAL provides migration path to new technologies
CA-TELON	PC workstation supports generation of mainframe, UNIX, AS/400 or PC programs	CA-Visual Objects for TELON provides migration path to new technologies, including generation of distributed applications with GUI-based front-end and mainframe- or midrange-based application server components
CA-REALIZER		Both a powerful language for end-user development and the common macro language across CA products
CA-C++		C++ provides object orientation for technical and system programming; CA-C++ provides a common language version across several platforms and CA-CommonView provides a common GUI platform for Windows, PM and Motif

CHAPTER 3

CA90s, The Supporting Architecture

CA Application Development Software is an integral part of CA90s: Computing Architecture For The 90s, which is the architectural foundation for the entire CA software product offering. CA90s is aimed at meeting real-world demands in the changing, multiple-platform computing environment of the 90s.

CA90s enables Computer Associates to systematically bring its broad range of solutions, covering all categories of software, to all appropriate computing platforms in a way that achieves unprecedented levels of automation, integration and portability. This is accomplished by employing a layered design that insulates software solutions from the complexities and technical requirements of a wide range of operating systems, hardware platforms, network requirements and end-user interfacing preferences. At the same time, it allows the software solutions to benefit from a wealth of invaluable, shared services.

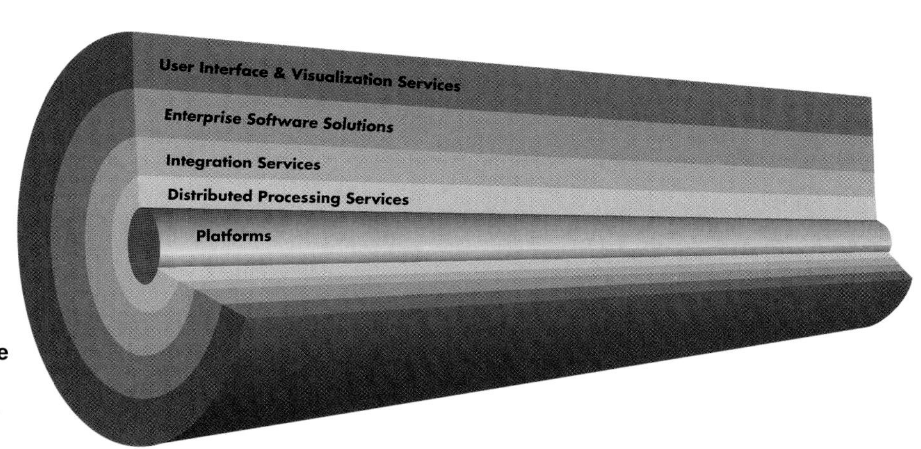

CA90s: Computing Architecture For The 90s is based on a layered architecture of uniform services that insulate enterprise solutions from the specific characteristics of each platform.

The Application Development Software uses most of the supporting services of CA90s, and in turn is the delivery vehicle that makes many of the services available to both CA and client developers. Some of the services have particular importance for application developers, and are described in depth here. For an overall description of the philosophy and components of CA90s, see the book *CA90s: Computing Architecture For The 90s, Third Edition*, available from CA.

Guiding Principles

CA90s consists of not only the structural design of a computing architecture, but also the underlying "guiding principles" of that design. These unique guiding principles have governed, and will continue to govern, new product development, technology acquisition and the enhancement of CA software, including the Application Development Software solutions:

- To optimize clients' investments in hardware, software and expertise, and build on those investments by enabling them to take advantage of emerging technologies
- To endorse and enhance established industry architectures and standards
- To promote the integration of software solutions across product families, operating systems and hardware platforms
- To enhance and extend distributed processing across multiple operating systems and hardware platforms
- To facilitate the portability of software solutions, engineered for efficiency on each platform

Each of these principles has direct relevance to application development systems.

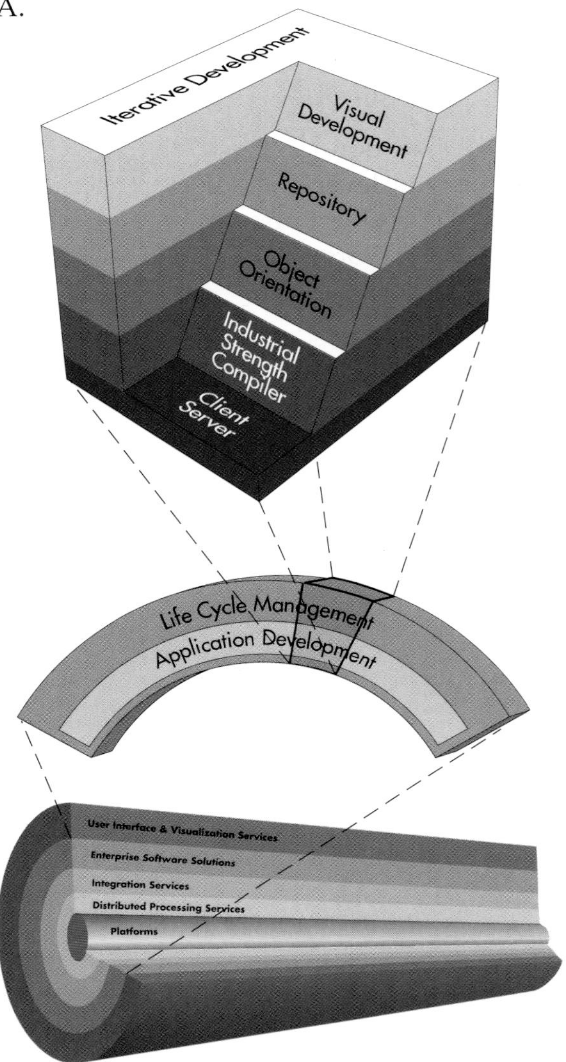

CA Application Development Software provides all of the tools needed for development, from technical services to life cycle management. The development systems rely on the technologies provided by CA90s Service Layers, and also act as the delivery vehicle to make these services available to clients.

Investment Protection And Leverage

Developers are directly exposed, every day, to the dilemma of how to exploit new technologies within a framework of existing technologies. It is easy to jump on new bandwagons, but anybody actually operating a business must consider continuity of programs and, perhaps more important, programmers. On the other hand, investments are not protected by staying away from new inventions. Technology is a perishable commodity. Unless existing investments are leveraged with new technology, they will eventually die.

CA Application Development Software, guided by the principle of investment protection and leverage, uniquely merges new technologies such as graphical user interface and object orientation with support for existing COBOL and Xbase programs and existing production databases.

Industry Standards

Support for industry standards is fundamental to the open architecture that enables CA Application Development Software to solve problems in all environments. The architecture is open at all levels, from operating systems, to database management systems, to CASE design tools, to compilers, to application level utilities. While CA Application Development Software forms a complete suite of tools, no developer is locked into using only CA tools. Major industry standards are directly supported, and major internal interfaces are public to allow extension of the systems to support specific proprietary technologies. In particular, see the discussion of database management systems in Chapter 4.

Integration Across Products, Operating Systems And Hardware Platforms

No application stands alone. As the world grows more complex, and pressures on cost-effectiveness heat up, the entire computing environment must be integrated. In particular, this means that application development tools must be integrated with systems management tools on each platform, and across platforms. CA90s provides a common set of integration services, including database, repository and security services, which lay the foundation for this integration of higher level tools.

Distributed Processing In Heterogeneous Environments

In an increasingly networked world, applications must be able to support distributed processing. To achieve this, first the development process itself must support distributed processing. Developers increasingly use workstations to offload development, workgroups need coordination across a network, and distributed applications need to be built and tested across a mixed network. The strongest combination is often a graphical workstation for the user interface and a powerful back-end processor for the real work—and if this is the right solution for transaction processing, it is also right for development, *ad hoc* query and reporting. All the development tools, at all levels, should support the distributed environment.

Multiple Platform Support

As an independent software vendor, CA has no allegiance to any specific operating systems or hardware platforms. As the industry goes through the radical shift to the mixed computing environment, CA90s is set to enable the restructuring of the entire IS process as required by the inexorable trends of the industry. Platform independence is granted by CA90s services, uniform across platforms, that insulate enterprise solutions from the idiosyncrasies of the different operating systems.

Application Development Software is the delivery vehicle for many of the services, and must provide the same uniform multiple-platform support to insulate developers from platform differences. The development systems support and exploit multi-platform capabilities on two levels: the development process may be offloaded from the target system to a workstation, and the generated applications can operate on multiple systems. Whichever platforms come to dominate the computing environment of the 90s, CA Application Development Software will be there to support it.

Key platforms targeted by CA90s include mainframes under MVS and VSE, midrange systems under UNIX, VAX/VMS, OS/400 and Tandem Guardian 90, and desktop systems under DOS, OS/2 and NT.

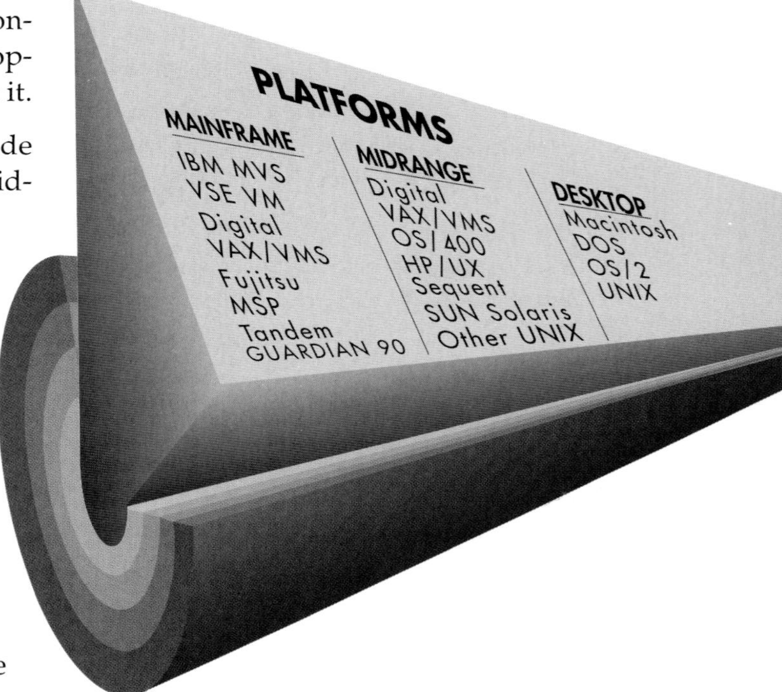

CA90s promotes portability of Enterprise Software Solutions across mainframe, midrange and desktop systems, as well as distributed processing within heterogeneous environments.

Service Layers

The major services that form the basis of the architecture are arranged in service layers between the enterprise solutions and the external environment. These layers insulate enterprise solutions, both those provided by CA and those built in-house by CA clients, from platform differences. They also provide higher level functions that improve the capabilities, consistency and cooperation of the solutions.

The service layers are:

- *User Interface and Visualization Services*

  This service layer provides the interface to the external world, including all aspects of the man–machine interface. Key services include user interfacing, graphics, image processing, printing and reporting, and voice interfacing. The application development tools provide the primary vehicle for delivering these services to developers, through technologies such as object orientation and visual development. Of course, the development tools themselves make heavy use of these services, for example to improve development productivity for mainframe applications, even if the application itself does not employ advanced user interfacing. The User Interface and Visualization Services—GUI, graphics and reporting—are described in Chapter 16.
- *Integration Services*

  This service layer provides functions that ensure coordination and integration among solutions. Key services include database management, repository management, event notification and security management. Several of these are of fundamental importance to application development and are discussed here, including the database management services in Chapter 4 and repository services in Chapter 13.
- *Distributed Processing Services*

  This service layer provides a wealth of higher level functions that insulate the enterprise solutions from the technical details of network protocols. The key services include database server, distributed database and cooperative processing, all built on the foundation of the Common Communication Interface. The Distributed Processing Services are discussed in depth in Chapter 15.

These services are used by many of the development tools discussed throughout this book—indeed, they lay the foundation for the distributed workbench and the distributed life cycle management facilities that are at the heart of many of the development tools.

Enterprise Software Solutions

The Enterprise Software Solutions layer consists of the Application Development Software that is the subject of this book, as well as Systems Management Software and Business Applications Software. These software solutions utilize the CA90s services to enhance integration, portability and ease of use. The benefits that accrue to the enterprise from this methodology increase geometrically as more enterprise solutions are implemented.

CA Systems Management Software provides a robust, distributed systems management model for all critical areas of enterprise computing. It includes: Automated Production Control; Automated Storage Management; Security, Control and Audit; Performance Management and Accounting; and Data Center Administration.

Systems Management Software is, of course, of fundamental importance to the security, integrity, reliability and availability of the entire operating environment. It effectively automates operations within a single system or across a heterogeneous network through a single point of administration. Some of the application development tools interface closely with systems management.

CA Business Applications Software addresses the entire business cycle, integrating specific business functions with advanced analytical capabilities. It covers both vertical and horizontal markets in such areas as Financial Management, Human Resource Management, Manufacturing Management, Distribution Management and Group Productivity.

The Business Applications directly use CA Application Development Software, and in many cases, the development tools are also provided to clients for extension and customization of the prepackaged business applications.

CHAPTER 4

Open Database Architecture

CA Application Development Software is based on an open database architecture with two key objectives: separating the database decision from the development system decision, and allowing the use of any major database, whether provided by CA or a third party.

Many application development systems force the choice of a database architecture. And in some cases the reverse is true, with the choice of a database forcing the choice of an associated development system. But in today's world of heterogeneous networked environments, no system can be a closed world. Applications need to cooperate, whether they are written in the same or different languages. And with the increasing use of client/server database architectures, applications need to cooperate from different platforms. For this reason, CA Application Development Software supports most major databases, without a forced association of language with database. This architecture allows developers to optimize each choice independently, to leverage their expertise, and to choose a development system based on the characteristics of the application, not the data.

CA90s provides database management services on all platforms, ranging from CA-DATACOM and CA-IDMS on mainframe, VAX, UNIX and PC-LAN systems, CA-DB on VAX and UNIX systems, and CA-Clipper and CA-dBFast on PC-LANs. The development systems obviously support these CA databases. The open development system architecture also supports major third-party Xbase and SQL databases, ranging from dBASE, FoxPro, Paradox and Btrieve to DB2, OS/2 DM, SQLServer and Oracle. This database independence protects client investments in databases, applications and expertise.

The development systems support different types of databases as appropriate, ranging from indexed files, through the Xbase DBF-style database, to navigational databases and relational SQL databases. They support major industry standard interfaces such as ANSI SQL, ANSI RDA, IBM DRDA and Microsoft ODBC. To ensure support for additional proprietary data sources, internal interface protocols are public, allowing third-party developers and clients to add interfaces.

This book focuses on the development systems and is not intended to describe the database solutions in detail. The overview below outlines how the application development systems interface to the various databases. Also note the discussion of client/server architectures in Chapter 15.

Open Architecture

The application development systems support standardized protocols for database drivers of different types. There are four major types of database drivers, identified by their access semantics:

- Xbase Data Manipulation Language (DML), supported by Replaceable Database Drivers (RDDs)
- SQL, supported through the CA Standard SQL Interface Service (CAISQI) which connects with major SQL standards
- Navigational database interfaces such as those for CA-IDMS and CA-DATACOM
- Various proprietary indexed file systems such as those for VSAM, RMS and Btrieve

Note that this grouping is based on the semantic philosophy of the access method, not on the implementation. From the application's viewpoint, all databases in the Xbase group, for example, provide similar facilities and support the same syntax, regardless of the underlying technology. While Xbase databases are traditionally implemented with DBF files using file sharing and record locking protocols, it is also possible to implement the Xbase semantics on a client/server database. Both implementations are semantically identical.

Similarly, SQL databases are essentially identical from the application's perspective, whether implemented on the same system or on a client/server or remote system. In addition, navigational database management access methods can be implemented on the same engine as relational access methods, allowing sharing of data between navigational legacy applications and relational query/reporting systems.

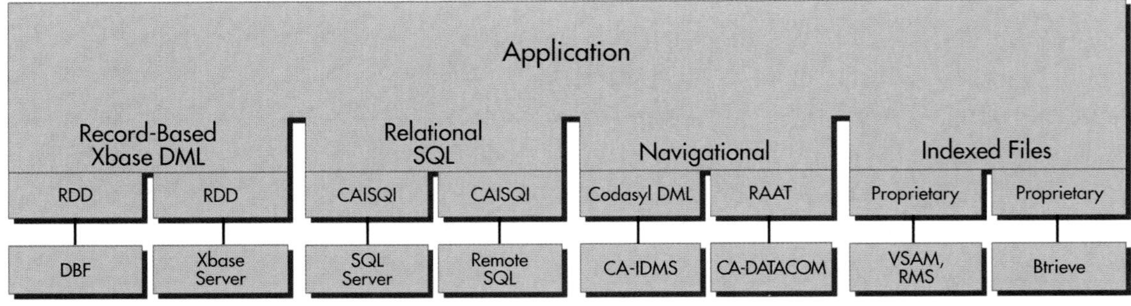

The CA open database architecture is based on plug-in database interfaces and standard protocols. The Replaceable Database Drivers (RDDs) support the Xbase Data Manipulation Language and drive different DBF types and other database engines. CAISQI interfaces to major SQL standards for relational database access, insulating the application from protocol differences in SQL standards. Proprietary protocols support high-performance navigational databases and simple indexed file systems. Some of the database engines (such as CA-IDMS and CA-DATACOM) may support more than one protocol simultaneously, with data sharing across access protocols.

Client/Server Databases

Xbase database systems and indexed file systems such as VSAM, RMS and Btrieve use a "file-sharing" architecture that places the database files on a shared server, but executes no code there—all database processing is done on the workstations. Database operations are coordinated and synchronized among users through a locking mechanism.

Because of its potential performance, scalability, integrity and security advantages, many users have increasing interest in the client/server architecture that executes the database code on the server. The ubiquitous "SQL-based relational client/server database" is generally viewed as the best candidate for this role. The question becomes, how can this database model be adapted to existing database designs, such as Xbase?

Two different approaches are possible: connecting the client/server database engine to the existing database syntax, such as Xbase DML, and explicitly accessing SQL directly from the language.

The choice of database access language should be viewed separately from the choice of implementation (file-sharing or client/server). Either implementation can support Xbase

Client/Server Database Architectures

Like many buzzwords, "client/server" is often used to mean different things. We use the term to mean a database architecture with significant database processing executing on the server.

The client/server model offers four important benefits: efficiency, scalability, integrity and security.

Efficiency: with a file-sharing mechanism, a lot of information is communicated back and forth between the workstations and the file server. In many cases, intermediate results not directly needed by an application are sent over the network to database code executing in the workstations. As the number of users on a network increases, the network traffic itself becomes a bottleneck.

In the client/server model, requests are sent to the server and only the desired data is returned to the workstation. Communicating at a higher level of abstraction reduces network traffic and increases overall application capacity.

In addition, since all database processing for all users executes on the same machine, there are more opportunities for clever caching of data. Today, when even 64Mb of RAM (often enough to cache an entire database!) is available for a few thousand dollars, this technique can significantly improve average throughput. But with a file-sharing database model, the clever caching tricks that perform so well in single-user configurations become counter-productive or inoperative with multiple simultaneous users. Only the client/server model can fully exploit today's and tomorrow's hardware.

Scalability: any system can become overloaded. With the client/server architecture, the capacity of the system can be incrementally increased by simply upgrading the server without changing the workstations. With a heterogeneous client/server database, the server can be a higher capacity system than a PC: RISC-based systems provide particularly strong price-performance, but Digital VAX and IBM AS/400 and mainframe systems offer other advantages.

Integrity: although not an inherent characteristic of the client/server architecture, extensive facilities for protecting the integrity of the data are integral to modern client/server databases. Transaction management with commit/rollback functions protect the data from destruction or inconsistency resulting from partially completed updates, even in the case of hardware or network failure.

Security: again not a characteristic of the client/server model per se, security facilities to protect the data from unauthorized access and accidental or malicious damage are a part of modern databases.

DML, for example, and either access language works with a client/server implementation. And similarly, a well-designed client/server engine can support multiple access languages, allowing simultaneous access through different methods.

Xbase-Style Databases

The Xbase DBF-style database convention is not well standardized. Although the basic database file format, the DBF file itself, is fairly consistent, the differences in indexing methods and locking protocols are such that applications written in the major dialects cannot reliably cooperate and share files. Not only can dBASE IV, CA-Clipper, CA-dBFast and FoxPro not cooperate, even dBASE III and dBASE IV are not compatible and cannot cooperate. The only good news is that CA-dBFast can cooperate with dBASE III without risk of conflict.

The differences are serious. The Xbase architecture allows indexes to become corrupted and indirectly cause corruption of data, without warning. The different locking protocols also mean that in a network with different Xbase systems operating, applications can step on each others' activities and corrupt data or lose transactions, again without warning. This lack of assured integrity means that incremental upgrading of a large network is very challenging: with traditional Xbase technology, all applications that share data must use the same language and database.

Replaceable Database Drivers

To alleviate this problem and bring order to the lack of standardization, CA-Clipper and CA-Visual Objects support plug-in database interfaces using the Replaceable Database Driver (RDD) architecture. This technology allows an enterprise to upgrade an application development system without having to abandon existing Xbase databases.

The RDD protocol supports the semantics of the standard Xbase DML. APIs are public, both for CA-Clipper under DOS and for CA-Visual Objects under Windows. This open database architecture allows third-party developers to extend the development systems with support for various database and file types.

Several standard RDDs from CA and third parties support a number of DBF variants and other databases:

- CA-Clipper style NTX index files (including conditional indexes)
- dBASE IV style MDX index files and dBASE III style NDX index files
- FoxPro style IDX index files
- Paradox databases
- Btrieve files (RDDs from third-party providers)

Note that these RDDs support non-DBF databases transparently from the Xbase DML syntax, and do not expose any proprietary syntax. Other tools can of course access the databases using any supported language.

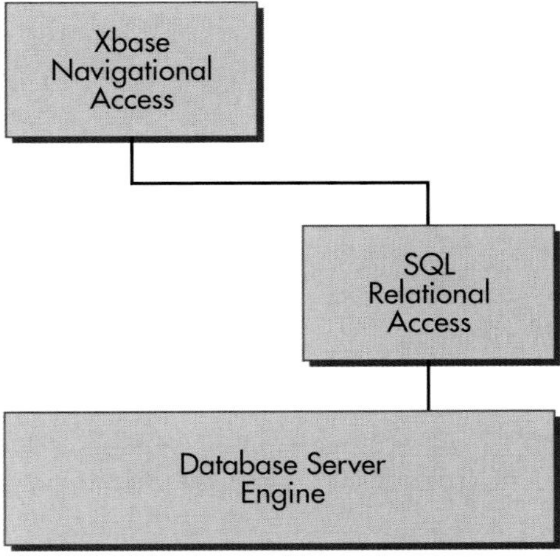

A recipe for failure: translating Xbase operations into SQL.

Client/Server Xbase Databases

Implementing Xbase DML on top of an "SQL-based relational database" poses several problems rooted in the paradigmatic incompatibility of the two database models, Xbase and SQL. Xbase is not a relational database model, it is a "navigational" database model which includes some operations that cannot be successfully translated into SQL. The result is either a complete failure to support certain Xbase operations, or slow performance caused by complex emulation structures.

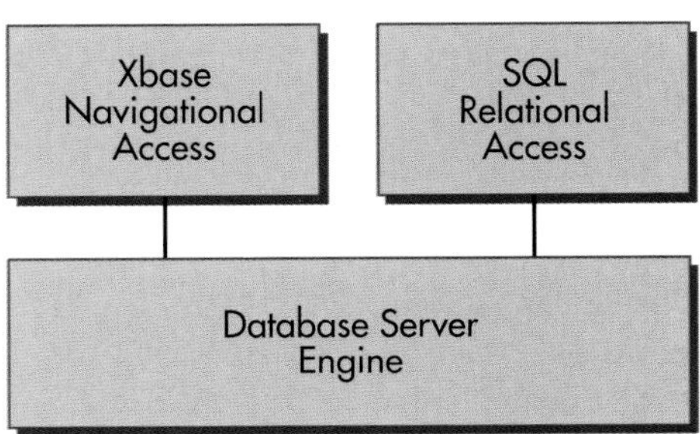

Xbase database operations and SQL accessing a common database engine as peers.

The solution lies in the fundamental observation that the relational model is not a prescription for how to build a database, but for how to talk to one. A well-designed database engine is not in itself relational, it is just a vehicle for managing data. The SQL processor is just an access method. A well-designed database engine can support many access languages.

Under this architecture, the navigational Xbase operations are on a peer level with the relational SQL operations. Both of them access the database engine directly, without any intermediary translation at runtime. Multi-user access is supported the same way that multi-user access is supported in any database. Transaction management (locking, deadlock resolution and rollback), referential integrity and security are provided by the engine, not by the access languages.

The Server Editions of CA-Clipper and CA-Visual Objects utilize this DML compatibility model to combine Xbase operations with the operational benefits of an industrial-strength database engine. The implementation uses the RDD architecture connected to a fully compatible interface for Xbase DML.

Some third-party database servers provide only relational access, and cannot support direct navigational access. In such cases where Xbase DML emulation would perform poorly, only explicit SQL access is provided.

SQL Databases

Industry Standard SQL Interfaces

CA Application Development Software supports industry standard SQL interfaces, including ANSI SQL, Remote Data Access (RDA) from ANSI and the SQL Access group, IBM DRDA and Microsoft ODBC. Through these interfaces, any conforming database management system is accessible.

While these industry standards have some syntactic and semantic differences, most major vendors are committed to converging on the evolving ANSI SQL standard.

Embedded Static SQL

Many of these standard interfaces are primarily aimed at query and reporting use, and support only dynamic access. The most robust way of accessing SQL from a programming language is "embedded SQL." With syntax and semantics defined by the ANSI standard, embedded SQL provides for input parameters in query conditions and update, insert and delete statements, and for the return of data and result codes to the program. Most importantly, embedded SQL supports "static" statements in addition to the "dynamic" statements commonly used in casual end-user query systems.

Static SQL statements are compiled at the time the program is compiled. This provides two important operational benefits: performance and security.

Performance of an SQL statement execution depends on query optimization. SQL is a high-level, nonprocedural language: it describes what data is to be accessed, not how to get to it. For complex queries, there may be several different ways of navigating the database, and the execution time may differ by several orders of magnitude between the most and the least efficient methods. It is the task of a query optimizer to select the best method, based on the form of the query, the indexes available, the statistical distribution of the data in the database, etc.

With dynamic SQL, the query is optimized every time it is executed. In production applications, it suffers from the same performance problem as interpretive languages. Static SQL compiles and optimizes the query only once; during execution, the precompiled query is retrieved and immediately run. If a precompiled query becomes invalid (for example, an index is dropped) the database management system automatically recompiles and re-optimizes it, with no involvement of either the developer or the end user. A developer can request a re-optimization if there is reason to believe the population statistics of the database have changed.

Security management is also stronger under static SQL. Consider a typical scenario: the data entry staff uses an application to enter purchase orders. The application contains logic to ensure that all information in the database is kept consistent: customer orders, deliveries, inventory, accounts receivable, etc. If the data entry staff has update privileges on all these tables, there is nothing to prevent them from accessing the database directly through an interactive front-end such as Query By Example and accidentally (or maliciously) damaging the data. With static SQL, the data entry staff need not have any privileges on the data tables, the *application* has update privileges on the tables and the data entry staff has only *execution* privileges on the application.

The development tools—COBOL, CA-ADS, CA-IDEAL, CA-TELON, CA-EASYTRIEVE, CA-RAMIS, and CA-Visual Objects—all support embedded SQL, both static and dynamic. The compilation of SQL statements is handled as an integral part of the compilation of an entire application. Xbase compatibility mode, navigational data access and embedded SQL may be used at the same time against the same data, with full protection of data integrity.

Database management systems supported with SQL access include DB2, CA-IDMS, CA-DATACOM, CA-DB, SQLServer, Oracle, Rdb and OS/2 Data Manager.

CA-IDMS/DB And CA-DATACOM/DB

In addition to their SQL access, the standard access methods for CA-IDMS and CA-DATACOM are of course navigational. These access methods are widely used in legacy systems and therefore are very important on downsizing platforms. They are also highly efficient and are better able to support high transaction rates than relational systems.

Both of these systems support complete SQL access to the same data managed by navigational methods, under the same architecture described above for Xbase: relational and navigational access methods are peers that both access the engine directly; neither access method is translated into the other. These access methods are available from CA-Realia COBOL, CA-ADS, CA-IDEAL and CA-Visual Objects for ADS and IDEAL.

Indexed File Systems

Most of the application development systems support various forms of indexed file systems, ranging from VSAM on mainframes, to RMS on VAX/VMS systems, to Btrieve on PC networks.

To support the migration of legacy applications to PC platforms, CA-Realia provides complete VSAM emulation on the PC. CA-TELON is capable of generating applications for VSAM, providing support for mainframe, DOS and OS/2 environments.

Both CA-Clipper and CA-Visual Objects support Btrieve file systems from the Xbase Data Manipulation Language (DML), by way of Replaceable Database Drivers (RDDs) for Btrieve.

Object-Oriented Access

All the database management systems have procedural access mechanisms. Within the object-oriented CA-Visual Objects structure, there is also a class library that provides an alternative way of dealing with the database, one more consistent with the object-oriented way of working with other entities. The database classes are also integrated closely with the GUI class library, providing automatic database lookup and validation, as well as direct browsing and editing.

SECTION II

Planning, Management And Design

Planning And Management Of The Development Process

Application development is not only a matter of technology. The management of the development and maintenance process is as important as the technical development itself. Schedules and resources, data elements and application components, release and distribution—all these aspects of the process need management tools that allow forecasting, planning, tracking, coordination, record keeping and auditing.

Project planning and management tools help the development manager estimate and plan project schedules and resource requirements, track and manage deliverables, schedules and resource allocations, and measure productivity.

Requirements analysis, functional specification and external and internal design are important steps in any development and maintenance activity. Today, these activities require not only traditional "front-end CASE" technology, but also support for an iterative development process. Modern development tools must provide for this model not only in the initial planning phase, but throughout the application life cycle.

Coordination among several developers and management of multiple components and versions are particularly important for larger, mission-critical applications. As both development and maintenance increasingly move to desktop workstations, the workgroup needs management tools that facilitate the communication and coordination that is an integral part of mainframe development systems. Without such tools, the convenience and productivity of the desktop environment carries an unacceptable price: breakdown of control.

Life cycle management tools provide necessary functions such as library management to keep track of all the components of the application, a data dictionary to keep track of the information processed, and version and release management to coordinate between various versions of various applications as they progress from development through testing to production.

The life cycle management tools also provide coordination between heterogeneous systems. They allow a development group to store work-in-progress in workstation and network libraries and use the mainframe as a central, enterprise-wide repository.

These planning and management tools are important for both maintenance of legacy systems and development of applications for the new environments. The tools described here are adapted to both categories of development systems. Their specific integration with legacy and new-technology systems is discussed in the context of those systems.

CHAPTER 5

Project Estimation, Planning And Tracking

Development managers often need to estimate the size, cost, resource consumption and risk of projects, both for new application development as well as for maintenance or enhancement of existing applications. Such estimates are at the heart of approval and funding decisions and of buy/build analysis. Without accurate estimates, development will not produce realistic budgets and completion dates, and will have no credibility with management and the user community. In practice, however, accurate estimates are rare because of a chicken-and-egg problem: the estimates need detailed design and plan information about the project, which is not available until well into the project life cycle, after funding approval.

However, reliable estimates on the duration and resource consumption of a project can be produced based on high-level information about the application and the organization, and on statistical analysis of past industry experience. This approach allows a development manager to evaluate different scenarios for the project during the early requirements specification phase.

Project planning is equally important, and is often neglected for similar reasons: it is cumbersome and enough information is not available early in the project. But without a plan, staffing assignments cannot be made, dates for deliverables are guesses, and dependencies on outside resources cannot be identified. Again, plans for typical business programming projects can be constructed based on industry experience and on answers to general questions about the characteristics of the project.

Progress must be carefully monitored during the development project. Project management technology lets the development manager track schedules and deliverables, identify the impact of schedule slippages, and interactively try out "mid-course corrections."

CA Application Development Software addresses the estimation, planning, tracking and measurement of the development process with an integrated suite of five strategic PC-based products: CA-FPXpert, CA-ESTIMACS, CA-PLANMACS, CA-SuperProject and CA-METRICS. Each tool may be used independently or in concert with the others.

Application Size Estimation

CA-FPXpert computes function points, a standard metric for expressing the size of an application regardless of the language or database used to implement it. Function points are a more universal method of sizing an application than lines of source code, which can vary greatly depending on the implementation language and programming style. CA-FPXpert helps development staff over the learning curve of using the function point technique, through an online "tutor." It also helps to ensure the consistency and accuracy of function point counting. CA-FPXpert conforms to the standard counting practices published by the International Function Point User Group. It integrates well with the formal design information gathered by the Information Engineering method, and with Entity-Relationship and Data Flow Diagrams.

Project Size And Cost Estimation

CA-ESTIMACS produces quick and accurate estimates for duration and resource consumption of a project during the requirements definition phase. It estimates the effort, time, cost, staffing, risk levels, financial benefits and portfolio impacts based on a statistical database of real-world projects, *without* the need for detailed project information. CA-ESTIMACS can use function point estimates but can also operate independently, producing estimates based on answers to 25 high-level questions about the project and the organization. It allows a development manager to do "what-if" evaluation of different project scenarios, such as design trade-offs, scope changes, different development approaches, changes in staffing level and time constraints. It also takes into account the level of experience of the staff on the project, the different degrees of efficiency achieved with small and large teams, etc. The underlying knowledge base, which is based on years of extensive statistical research of over 13,000 projects, provides the basis for accurate and consistent project estimates.

Project Plan Generation

CA-PLANMACS builds a development plan based on project information and standard project planning templates. If the development group follows a standard methodology, whether developed in-house or acquired from an outside vendor, the tasks and deliverables specified by the planning template method may be used to automatically build detailed project plans for various types of projects. The output from CA-PLANMACS is a detailed plan that includes phases, tasks and activities, and a complete work breakdown structure.

Planning And Monitoring

CA-SuperProject is a powerful project management system that supports both GUI and character-based environments. It uses the graphical user interface to simplify the specification and analysis of task dependencies and resource allocation. Project management technology lets the development manager track schedules and deliverables, identify the impact of schedule slippages using critical path analysis and detailed resource-limited scheduling, and interactively try out "mid-course corrections" by specifying and analyzing task dependencies and resource allocation.

Supporting both PCs and midrange systems, CA-SuperProject combines convenient planning, tracking and analysis tools for project leaders with consolidation of multiple subplans into a larger project-wide plan.

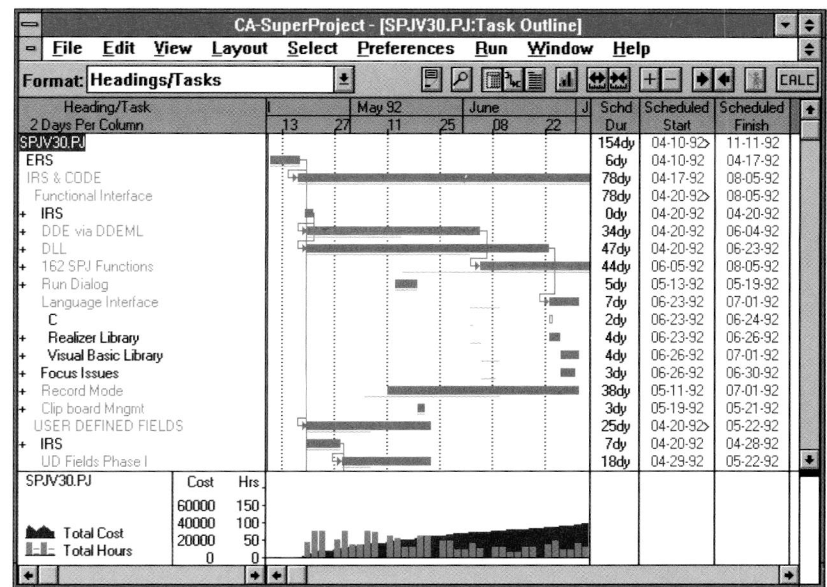

CA-SuperProject uses a graphical user interface to facilitate and streamline the planning, tracking and management of development projects. A development manager can evaluate the impact of changed schedules and resource allocations when planning "mid-course" corrections.

Measurement

CA-METRICS provides facilities for building, maintaining and analyzing a database of software development metrics that can be used to evaluate the impact on productivity of introducing new tools and methods. It provides facilities for measuring progress from project to project and to compare performance with the rest of the industry. It also provides defect tracking and analysis.

Integration

These tools form an integrated suite for managing the entire development process. CA-FPXpert produces function point estimates; its output may be used to feed CA-ESTIMACS, which estimates project duration and resource consumption; its output may be used to feed CA-PLANMACS, which produces a detailed task list; the output from CA-PLANMACS may be used as input to CA-SuperProject for scheduling and resource allocation. Finally, CA-METRICS can import information from CA-ESTIMACS, CA-FPXpert and CA-SuperProject, and act as the repository for development statistics for an IS organization.

Together, these planning and management tools allow a development manager to gain control of schedules, costs and resources. This not only benefits the development organization from a business viewpoint, it also serves to strengthen the credibility of the development organization and improve relationships with the end-user community. As much as prototyping and the new iterative development paradigm, robust planning and control are essential to making application development a proactive partner in the business of the enterprise.

CHAPTER 6

Requirements Analysis And Design

Over the years, different schools of thought have evolved in the areas of requirements analysis and design. Some developers emphasize formal methods with meticulous documentation of every step in the development life cycle. Others prefer rapid development techniques with a strong emphasis on prototyping and end-user involvement.

CA clients report different views on the relative merits of these techniques, based on their different needs and experiences. Overall, there is an emerging consensus that many of the analysis and design techniques promulgated by the industry have not been successful. Current trends seem to move away from the "control" approach, the attempt to manage complexity by dotting every "i" and crossing every "t." It appears that the approach of managing complexity through tight control, rigid formalism, and meticulous specification and documentation may be better suited to a more static environment than to today's competitive and fast-moving world. To be successful in meeting the rapidly evolving needs of the 90s, analysis and design must be based on a development paradigm that recognizes changing requirements and environmental conditions as a natural and inevitable part of life.

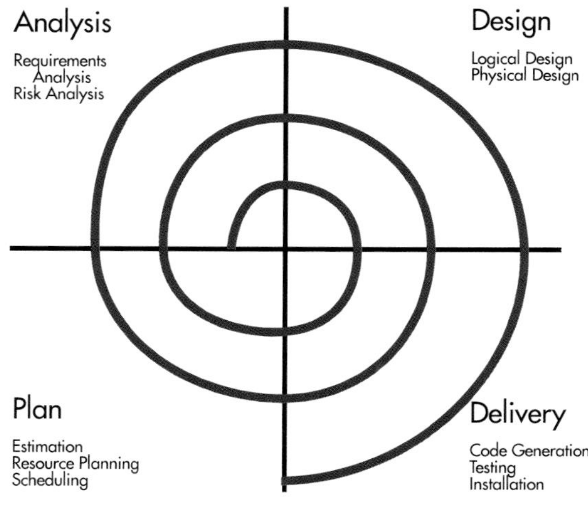

The "spiral life cycle" with its emphasis on iterative refinement during the life of the application appears more appropriate to the business needs of the 90s.

Instead of the classical "waterfall" life cycle, many developers today favor an iterative approach with strong involvement by end users, using prototyping and stepwise refinement of functioning models of the application. The iterative approach as illustrated in the "spiral life cycle" does not proceed linearly from requirements analysis, through design to coding and implementation. Instead it proceeds by building up an application's functionality from an initial concept or simulation, to more and more robust prototypes, to a functional solution. Design does not end with a "final product"—software development and maintenance is a matter of ongoing evolution, and successful tools and techniques must support this process.

In order to meet the need for rapid, responsive development, CA has concentrated its efforts on "back-end CASE," software engineering tools that actually expedite the construction and modification process: application generators, high-level languages and nonprocedural systems, visual development systems and object orientation. These tools provide integral support for prototyping and stepwise refinement.

Front-End CASE Integration

Many development organizations have made significant training investments in CASE methodologies and have achieved great benefits from the coordinated use of front-end CASE tools.

One of the practical problems that sometimes keep otherwise successful front-end CASE tools from achieving the productivity improvements expected is a lack of integration with the rest of the life cycle. As long as the analysis and design tools are isolated, all they produce is a lot of paper that must be transferred manually to the actual implementation. Not only is this inefficient, it is subject to interpretation errors that can have serious effects when several developers cooperate on a project. Automated integration between front-end and back-end CASE tools, databases and other development facilities can improve the reliability and efficiency of the process immeasurably.

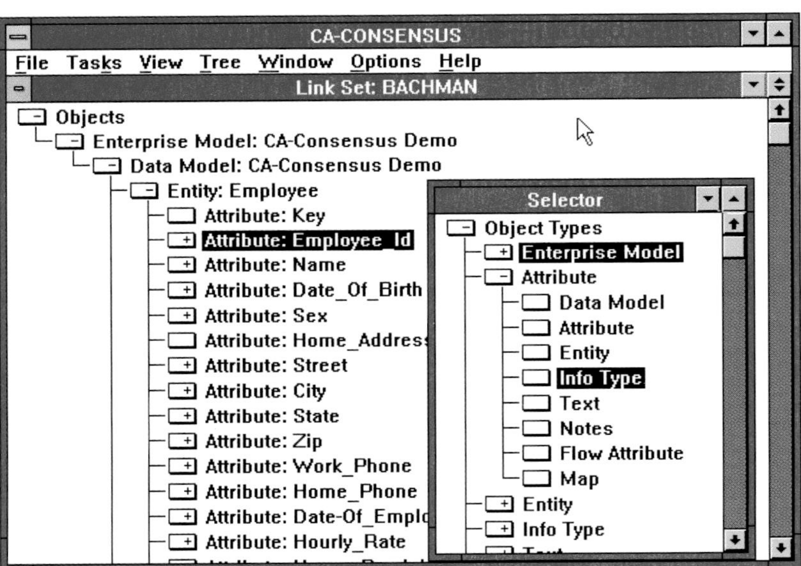

CA-CONSENSUS integrates leading front-end CASE tools with CA back-end CASE tools such as application generators and databases, integrating the entire application development process from analysis and design to code construction.

To support and integrate front- and back-end CASE tools, CA-CONSENSUS and CA-CASELINK provide links between major front-end CASE tools, including the Bachman, KnowledgeWare and InterSolv systems, and CA development systems such as CA-TELON, CA-IDMS/CA-ADS and CA-DATACOM/CA-IDEAL.

Iterative Development And Prototyping

Iterative development techniques, such as Rapid Application Development (RAD) and Joint Application Design (JAD), involve the end users in the design, specification and even implementation of the system.

These techniques require high-level development tools that allow rapid turnaround during evaluation of changes. Many developers use interpretive tools for prototyping, ranging from nonprocedural systems such as CA-QbyX and CA-RET to high-end languages combined with visual development tools, for example BASIC systems such as CA-REALIZER and Xbase systems such as CA-dBFast.

But interpreters are usually inadequate for the final production implementation, due to poor performance and weak integrity because of a lack of compile-time checking. This means that the prototype is discarded in the evolution to a production implementation ("throw-away prototyping"), in most cases preserving nothing more than documentation to aid the next step. Not only is this forced reimplementation of the system wasteful, it does not match the long-term iterative life cycle: in later iterations, there is no connection between the production system and the prototype for the next generation.

A truly effective system for iterative development should provide for prototyping, incremental refinement and production within a single system, integration through a common implementation technology and a common repository. A combination of visual development tools with object-oriented technology and a repository-based environment can provide such a strong foundation for iterative development, as demonstrated by CA-Visual Objects. The visual development tools permit the creation of "mock-up" prototypes that show the appearance and perhaps navigation of the system, and a seamless progression into a "functional prototype" through iterative refinement. The object-oriented compiler provides an automatic "make" facility with very fine granularity, combining the immediate turnaround of an interpretive system with a natural migration to the compiled production system.

The visual development system integrates a high-level language that permits very loose and informal development. It supports "late binding," undeclared and untyped variables that are dynamically allocated at runtime. It also supports the strict typing and scoping required to assure the performance and integrity of a production system. By permitting a mix of formal and informal styles, CA-Visual Objects provides a direct evolution from prototype to production, through an evolution of the program from late- to early-binding. The ability to prototype and implement in the same system provides natural support for the iterative life cycle. Extensions and modifications may be prototyped directly into the production version, and later refined to the next generation production version.

When the target application includes existing code written in traditional 3GLs such as COBOL, a hybrid system is the best choice. CA-Visual Objects allows quick and informal creation of prototypes that invoke legacy code where appropriate. This system offers the best of both worlds: the responsiveness required of a prototyping system, a smooth transition to the production system, and an effortless movement back to the prototyping environment for the next iteration.

CA-Visual Objects, the main enabling technology for the iterative development process, is described in detail in Section IV, Chapters 11 through 14. It provides a number of language flavors: CA-Visual Objects for Clipper, dBFast, dBASE and FoxPro provide an Xbase-style language, while CA-Visual Objects for COBOL, ADS, IDEAL and TELON provide a natural migration path for mainframe developers.

CHAPTER 7

Life Cycle Management

All development and maintenance projects need robust tools for management of libraries, repositories and the life cycle in general. On every development platform, these tools need to provide the control and integrity that is essential for mission-critical applications, especially for maintenance and enhancement of legacy systems that are already deployed. By definition, a mission-critical application is one for which the slightest disruption is costly or harmful and, in either case, unacceptable.

Today, with the continuing evolution from centralized, mainframe-based to distributed, multi-platform development, the need for effective control of the entire application is magnified. Life cycle management now entails a far more complex series of tasks, presenting ample opportunity for costly errors. Indeed, the danger of loss of control, security and integrity is one of the major barriers to downloading development and maintenance of legacy applications to desktop and network systems.

A robust solution for distributed life cycle management must provide the key functions of *library management, version management, configuration management, turnover management* and *release management* across a heterogeneous networked environment. It should provide "single-image" control of all application components and all steps in the life cycle.

Library Management

Software is an asset that must be protected against unauthorized access and change, whether malicious or unintentional. Library management ensures that the right people have access to the source and object modules that support the business. CA-LIBRARIAN and CA-PANVALET provide reliable security through check-in and check-out, change auditing and reporting, and cataloging.

Version Management

With many different programmers working on several different releases of a software application, it is critical that the various changes made to software modules are tracked, controlled and managed. Version management is the ability of the library management system to simultaneously manage several different versions of the same software module. CA version control systems accomplish this by storing the differences between the original version of a software module and a revised version. This not only saves space, but also makes it possible to determine the specific changes made to any software module, who made the changes and when the changes were made.

Configuration Management

Most bugs that result in system failures are caused by using incompatible versions of modules in the system. An application is usually composed of many different components: software modules, copylib members, object modules and procedures. Each of these can have different versions or be at different stages of completeness. Configuration management allows a complete release of a software application to be built with compatible versions of its component parts.

This facility includes a user-configurable "make" facility capable of creating jobs for all aspects of building an application, including JCL generation for compilation, preprocessing, DB2 binding and other database operations.

Turnover Management

When an application goes into production, it is critical that all the component parts have been tested and documented, and are included in the final system that will be turned over to users. CA turnover management software automates this detail-oriented task and ensures that all the component parts of a system are promoted together from one release level to the next.

Release Management

In the highly centralized world of mainframe computing, most users have access to the same copy of an application's software and use it in the same operating environment. In desktop and network environments, however, users can have access to different versions of the same application and can run it in vastly different environments. To provide the level of support and service end users expect, it is critical to control where and how users are running applications. Release management helps support and control software distribution, version upgrades and machine configurations in networked environments.

Distributed Environments

As developers increasingly offload development and maintenance to workstations and networks, the management of assets and resources becomes more difficult. But the distributed development environment must retain the level of integrity already established on mainframe systems.

CA Application Development Software accomplishes this with CA-PAN/LCM, a network life cycle management system for support of all development tools, from COBOL to Xbase and the object-oriented CA-Visual Objects systems. CA-PAN/LCM provides synchronization among the members of the development workgroup and management of application versions, configurations and releases.

CA-PAN/LCM integrates with mainframe library management systems such as CA-LIBRARIAN and CA-PANVALET; it also supports storage of programs in ordinary partitioned data sets. It provides automatic upload and download of application components, with the appropriate check-out/check-in synchronized correctly.

The distributed life cycle management system addresses the entire application control process, automatically generating JCL for mainframe build procedures with the selective regeneration of an automatic "make" facility.

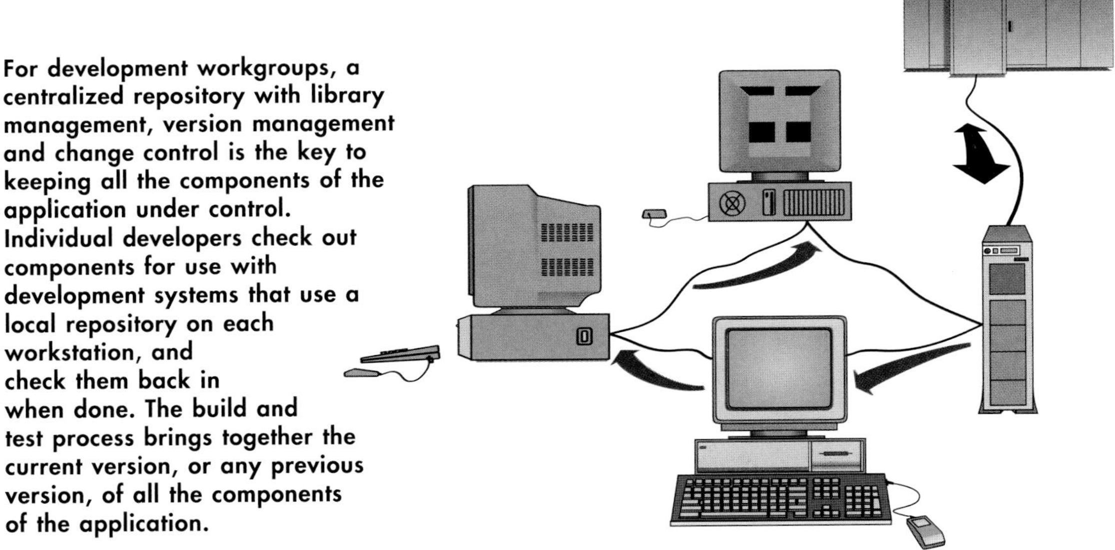

For development workgroups, a centralized repository with library management, version management and change control is the key to keeping all the components of the application under control. Individual developers check out components for use with development systems that use a local repository on each workstation, and check them back in when done. The build and test process brings together the current version, or any previous version, of all the components of the application.

Object-Oriented Repository

The iterative, visual development tools of the CA-Visual Objects development environment are based on an object-oriented repository that acts as an application dictionary and library. This repository is closely integrated with the development tools, aiding the developer with very high bandwidth communication. It can immediately bring up complete information about a referenced entity, such as the formal parameter specification of a function, use and dependency relationships, and the inheritance hierarchy of a class. It can optionally display the complete definition of any entity such as a function or type declaration whenever the mouse cursor moves over the entity in one of the repository browsers, and to automatically fill in function prototypes in the source editor.

It also drives the automatic "make" facility that is at the heart of the fine-grained, entity-level incremental compilation facility. The CA-Visual Objects repository is much more than just a data dictionary or application library, it is an active development tool closely integrated with the entire development process.

Coordination of developer workgroups, with version management, change control and check-out/check-in facilities, are provided through technology from CA-PAN/LCM.

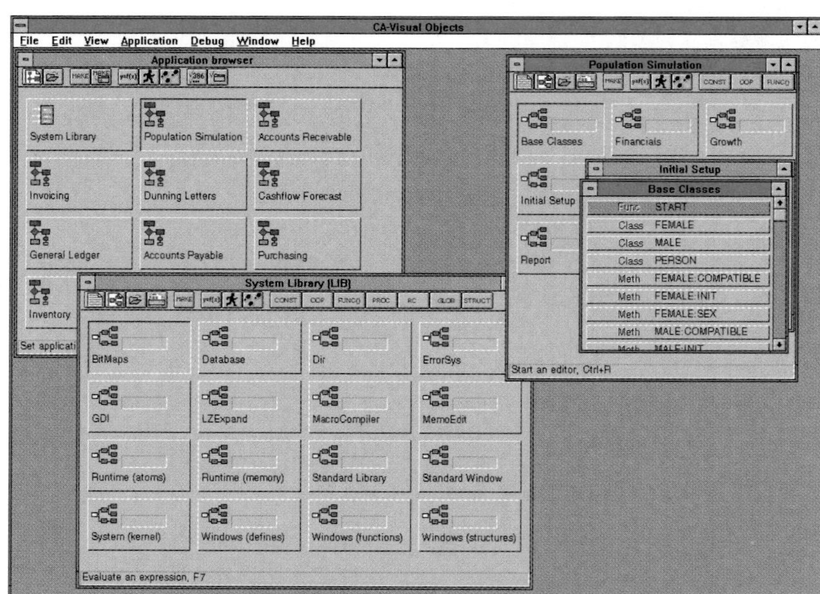

The development environment for the CA-Visual Objects systems is based on an object-oriented repository, which is used to store all entities that constitute an application. This repository is intimately integrated with the development tools, from editors and painters to the compiler and "make" facility.

SECTION III

Legacy Systems

Development And Maintenance Of Legacy Applications

To help mainframe developers take advantage of the power and responsiveness of desktop workstations and the high price-performance of midrange systems, CA Application Development Software provides languages and tools for offloading development and maintenance of legacy applications to PC, network, UNIX and VAX systems.

The languages most commonly used in mainframe development are COBOL, CA-ADS and CA-IDEAL; CA-TELON is the leading application generator. Systems such as CA-EASYTRIEVE and CA-RAMIS are frequently used for reporting and other tasks. These systems are all available in the form of PC development workstations, fully compatible with the mainframe.

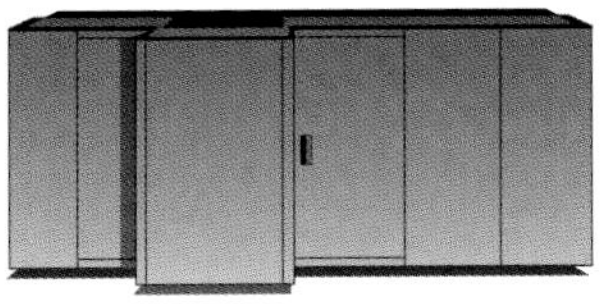

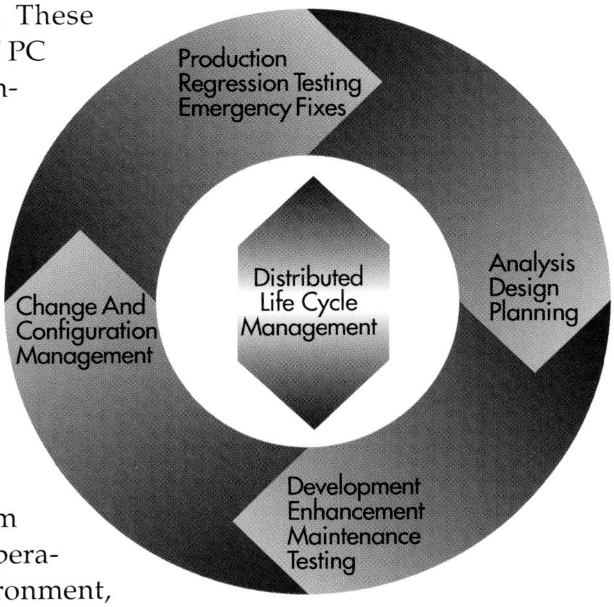

For downsizing to midrange systems, the languages and supporting databases are also available in UNIX and VAX versions. CA-TELON can generate UNIX and Tandem applications.

A workstation with a graphical user interface optimizes the productivity of development and maintenance. It provides visual representation of system analysis and debugging, based on cooperative processing with the target environment, whether a mainframe, a UNIX system or a PC-LAN environment.

The graphical workstation provides a distributed development environment that integrates networks, midrange systems and mainframes for development, analysis and debugging of COBOL programs. The workstation exploits the graphical user interface and the multitasking environment to present the structure of the COBOL program and debugging information in the clearest possible way, fully integrated

A distributed development and maintenance environment for legacy applications addresses all aspects of the application life cycle. It integrates mainframes, midrange systems, networks and workstations, with each phase placed on the platform most appropriate to the task. A graphical workstation visualizes application structure and runtime information. Distributed life cycle management protects the integrity of the application.

with the execution system. Complete life cycle management facilities provide version control, change and configuration management, and automatic release generation, again across multiple platforms.

Growth Path To New Technologies

Section III discusses legacy applications with their traditional user interface structure—either 3270-style block mode or character mode—even if they are migrated to smaller platforms such as PCs, LANs, UNIX, VAX/VMS and Tandem systems. The growth path to graphical user interfaces and object-oriented programming lies in the CA-Visual Objects system, described in Section IV, Chapters 11 through 16.

CHAPTER 8

Development And Maintenance

Mainframe legacy systems are migrating to other platforms in three steps: offloading development and maintenance of applications intended for mainframe execution, downsizing production execution, and exploiting new technologies. Developers need supporting tools on workstations, networks and midrange systems: development, analysis, test execution and debugging tools for step one, compatible production runtime support for step two. Complete compatibility and an understanding of the original mainframe environment are essential for successful migration. (Step three is discussed in Section IV.)

As the development and maintenance life cycie for mainframe applications is increasingly offloaded to desktop workstations, management of the distributed environment becomes a demanding task. Developers need tools that administer resources across the systems, and that handle the practical aspects of editing and testing a program on one system and delivering it on another: file transfer, JCL generation, recompilation, file management, etc. Ideally, support tools should optimize operation for a distributed environment by transparently placing individual functions on the platform most suited to the task.

The right tool for offloading development and maintenance is a distributed development workbench that integrates the platforms; provides distributed library management; ensures the continued integrity of the application with distributed life cycle management facilities providing version and configuration management; provides fully compatible multi-platform compilers and runtime support; provides distributed testing and analysis; and does all this transparently from one user interface framework, regardless of which target systems are used.

Distributed COBOL Workbench

The complete suite of facilities for construction, maintenance, analysis, debugging, testing and life cycle management of COBOL programs is integrated under the CA-Realia II distributed workbench. These separate functions are integrated into a single development and maintenance environment that presents the developer with a single user interface, a single view of the world and a single source of control. This single image provides uniform operation regardless of whether programs are stored, executed, debugged or analyzed on a mainframe, on the same workstation or on other PCs in the network.

The library management functions check programs in and out across the network, extracting as necessary from mainframe libraries and storing them on the network or workstation. Editing is done on the workstation with a GUI-based source code editor. An automatic "make" facility utilizes the CA-Realia compiler to generate the program for execution on the workstation. For mainframe applications, a similar "make" facility generates JCL for compilation, linking and binding on the mainframe.

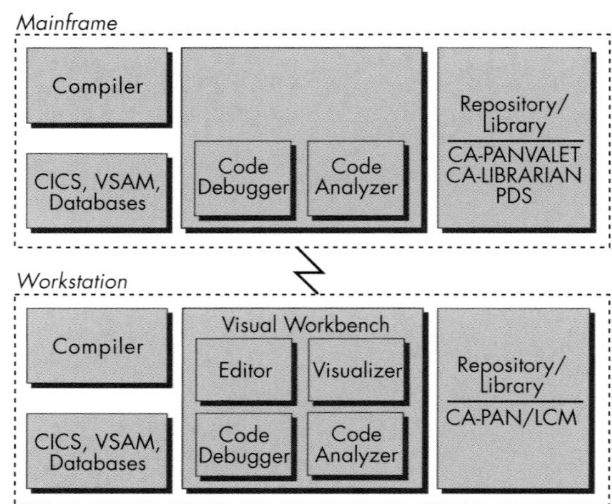

The development, maintenance, testing and life cycle management facilities work together to produce a distributed workbench that looks the same to the developer whether programs are stored, compiled, analyzed, executed or debugged on the mainframe or workstation.

The CA-COBOLVISION analysis and debugging facilities are visually presented on the workstation, with the back-end analyzer (see Chapter 9) and debugger (see Chapter 10) integrated with the compiler and execution environment on either mainframe or workstation.

The runtime environments are compatible across the two platforms, including full support for CICS, VSAM, IMS DL/I, CA-IDMS and CA-DATACOM. The final application may be left in the PC-LAN environment for downsized production execution, or brought back up to the mainframe for execution there.

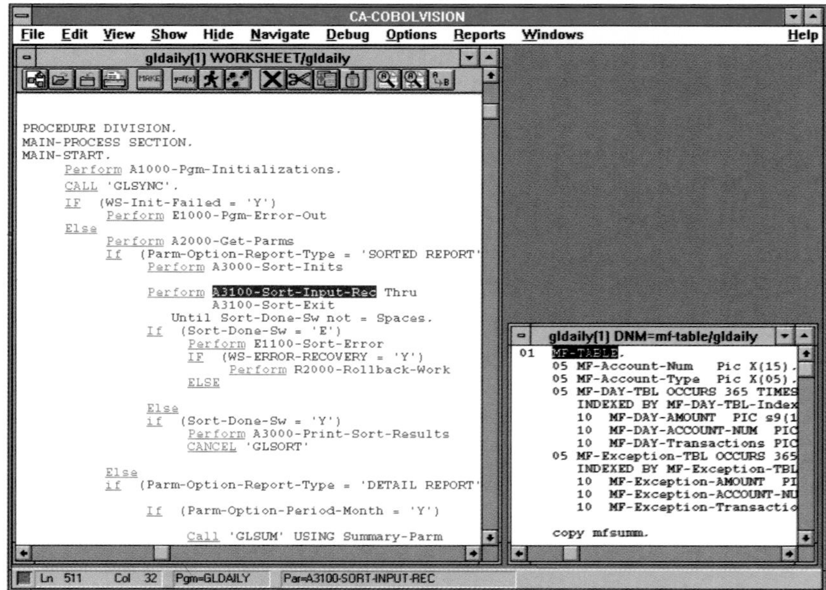

The CA-Realia II development workbench presents editor, life cycle manager, debugger and analyzer under a common graphical framework.

Library Management

The workbench fully integrates the distributed library management facilities of CA-PAN/LCM, CA-PANVALET and CA-LIBRARIAN. (Mainframe PDSs are also supported for sites that do not use integrated library management systems.) The developer can perform key library functions from inside the workbench environment, such as checking programs in and out and downloading them from mainframe to workstation or vice versa.

Integrating Multiple Systems

The workbench provides a consistent environment that can simultaneously integrate multiple target systems. This allows developers to edit, compile, execute and debug on several systems, all with a single, consistent user interface.

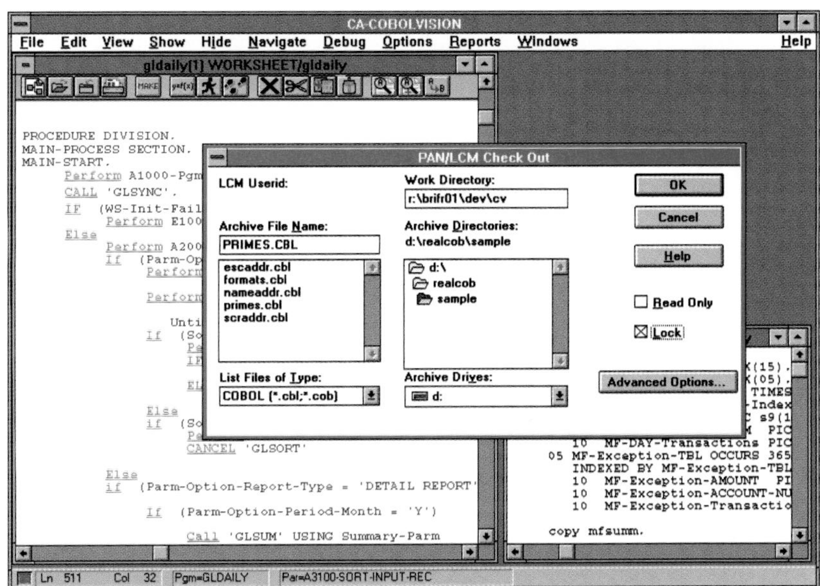

The development workbench provides integrated facilities for checking application components in and out of the CA-PAN/LCM network-based library.

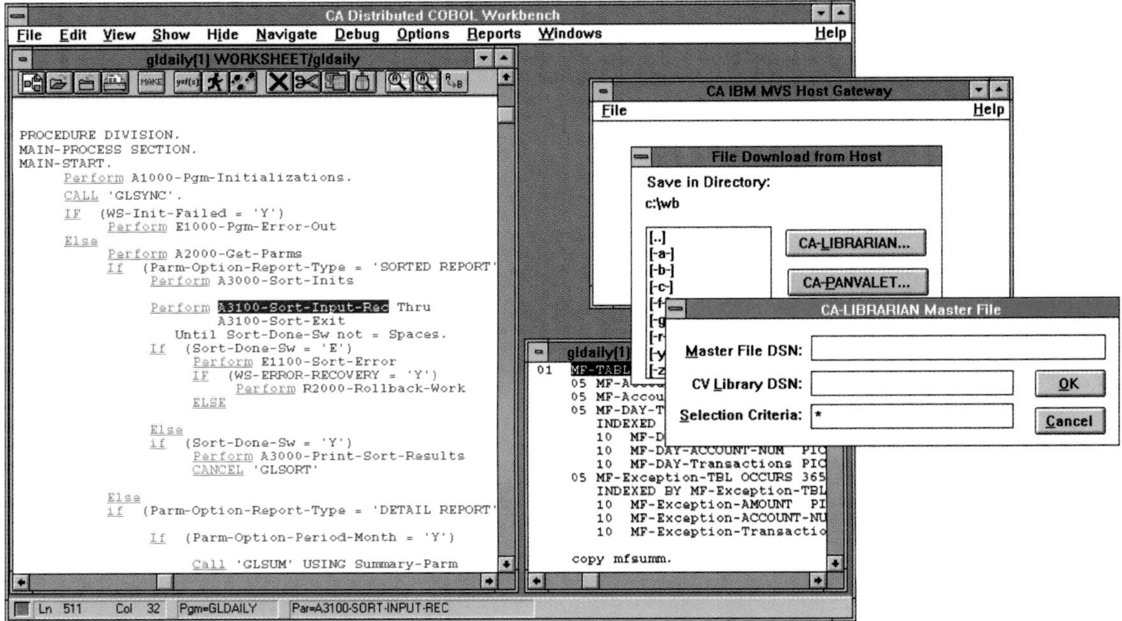

The development workbench integrates directly with mainframe library management systems, providing remote check-in and check-out and background upload/download.

The multitasking nature of the GUI environment allows developers to compare several executing programs, analyze source code, download code from a mainframe library and do many other things, all without interrupting the individual sessions. The dynamic execution behavior of a program on the different systems may be compared, with full interactive debugging capabilities in all target environments.

The distributed development systems and life cycle management systems are built on the Common Communication Interface (CAICCI), which provides uniform links across a multitude of platforms. Techniques for incorporating distributed processing technology in applications are discussed in Chapter 15.

Application Generator

CA-TELON is the dominant application generator for online, batch and server programs. It generates COBOL and PL/I applications, targeted for mainframe, AS/400, UNIX (HP-UX, AIX and others), Tandem and PC (DOS and OS/2) systems. Environment support includes CICS and IMS/DC, including CICS OS/2. The generated code is designed for any one of a number of databases, including DB2, IMS DL/I, CA-IDMS, CA-DATACOM and VSAM on mainframes; the native database as well as SQL/400 on the AS/400; Oracle, Sybase, CA-DB on UNIX systems; Nonstop SQL on the Tandem; and Btrieve, IBM OS/2 DM, CA-DB, SQLServer and Oracle for DOS and OS/2.

The CA-TELON development environment operates on mainframes under MVS, and on PCs as the CA-TELON PWS workstation under DOS and OS/2. Through its integration with CA-CONSENSUS, CA-TELON provides a continuous bridge from high-level design in front-end CASE tools to program generation. See Chapter 14 for information on the future growth path of CA-TELON into the world of graphical user interfaces and client/server applications.

4GL Development Tools

The fourth-generation development system for the CA-IDMS database is CA-ADS and the integrated development environment centered around the IDD dictionary. Similarly, the 4GL for CA-DATACOM is CA-IDEAL and its dictionary. Together with COBOL, these systems are available on PC, network and midrange (UNIX and VAX) systems. Providing fully compatible operation and a consistent development environment, CA-ADS and CA-IDEAL are highly suitable for offloading development as well as downsizing execution.

Similarly, CA-EASYTRIEVE and CA-RAMIS are available as fully compatible PC workstations, with access to mainframe legacy databases through server components.

These systems all support the new technologies, both GUI environments (see Chapters 14 and 16) and client/server configurations (see Chapter 15).

CHAPTER 9

Program Analysis

Studies have shown that as much as 80 percent of all MIS activity is spent performing maintenance on existing COBOL applications. Any technique that improves the effectiveness and productivity of this maintenance burden can have a profound influence, directly by making maintenance more responsive and reliable, and indirectly by freeing more resources to new application development.

Perhaps more insightful than just the magnitude of the maintenance effort is seeing how it is divided. Studies have shown that rather than "bug-fixing" (corrective maintenance) and "adding features" (perfective maintenance), the vast majority of all so-called maintenance work consists of adapting applications to changes in the environment. This adaptive maintenance ranges from upgrades of operating systems, compilers and other utilities, to changes in file formats or database technology; it also includes interfacing existing applications with new ones, whether built in-house or acquired.

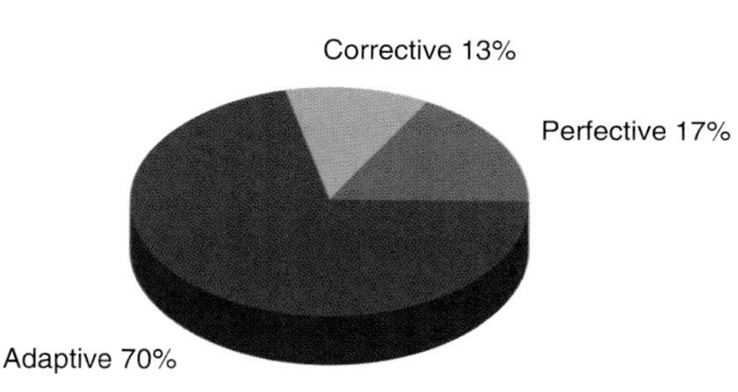

The IS maintenance burden, which may be up to 80 percent of all IS activity, is dominated by adapting applications to changes in the environment.

This last component, integration of legacy systems with new applications, will become increasingly important and increasingly challenging as the environment becomes more complex, with multiple platforms, distributed processing, and "surrounding" mainframe legacy systems with GUI workstations.

The key to all maintenance, but especially to the adaptive maintenance that dominates maintenance costs, is understanding the structure of the systems being maintained. CA-COBOLVISION is a workstation- and mainframe-based tool that enables graphical, detailed and accurate analysis of COBOL programs, regardless of their age or complexity, providing a solid foundation for the ongoing maintenance process.

Visualizing Program Structure

Only the very smallest COBOL programs are easy to visualize, and mission-critical line-of-business applications are neither small nor simple. Whether maintaining, updating or migrating existing programs, programmers spend much of their time trying to visualize the complex structure of large programs. With the advent of newer COBOL '85 constructs such as the nesting of programs, it has become even more difficult to visualize where one program's sphere of influence ends and another begins. Even well-structured programs can become difficult to understand when nested PERFORMs necessitate paging back and forth between references to performed blocks of code. And many of the crucially important programs that run today's enterprises are old and not well structured.

Even from a mechanical viewpoint, keeping track of the interrelationships among program components is cumbersome. Most programmers are reduced to using such tools as paper clips and colored pens to mark up program listings.

The analytical and presentation power of computer systems is eminently capable of assisting in visualizing these relationships. It is possible to do better than a cross-reference listing. Dynamic, interactive systems have proven their value in browsing information with complex interrelationships.

Challenging analysis tasks required for most kinds of maintenance include:

- "Seeing the forest for the trees"—reducing the clutter to reveal the major components of a system hidden among all the implementation details
- Following the execution thread through a complex program forward and backward as it jumps among paragraphs and subprograms
- Identifying the actual modular program structure—those logical groupings of code and data that operate as (more-or-less) independent components, and their relationships
- Identifying code module interdependence, direct or indirect
- Identifying data interdependence, direct or indirect, among paragraphs, subprograms and other modular structures
- Identifying "dead code" that is never executed (often remnants from previous versions)

Managing Complexity

Most line-of-business programs perform very complex tasks and necessarily have very complex structure. In addition, programs that have grown and evolved over several years often accumulate growths that obscure their essential organization and processing logic. Documentation may be incomplete or out of date. Without a sense of global visibility and understanding of the program structure, the implementation of enhancements and fixes to existing programs is difficult and time-consuming. It is also error-prone, causing not only processing errors that must be tracked down, but also adding to the accumulation of logic debris.

Many IS organizations have some very complex programs that no one has touched in years for fear of causing new and potentially bigger problems. This legitimate "fear of the unknown" can be overcome only by a more complete understanding of how the programs actually operate. Automated logic analysis tools such as CA-COBOLVISION make it possible to tackle these complex programs.

Distributed Program Analysis And Visualization

COBOL program analysis is by its very nature an interactive and resource-intensive process, ill suited to the characteristics of the mainframe. Mainframe-based tools are also severely limited by the presentation of information on 327x terminals. Complex information, such as the control and data structures of a real-world program, cries out for graphical presentation, similar to what a programmer does with marker pens and a desktop workstation can do with GUI technology. On the other hand, if the program is managed on a mainframe system, it is logical to analyze it there, to ensure that the right versions of all program components are being analyzed. A dilemma: there are benefits to doing the analysis on both sides. The most powerful and cost-effective solution is to share the processing between the mainframe and a workstation, making each responsible for the tasks that it handles most efficiently and effectively.

CA-COBOLVISION uses this distributed architecture to great benefit. Its mainframe component performs the analysis of the program from source files and compiler output while the workstation handles all user interaction and presentation.

Host Program Analysis

CA-COBOLVISION analyzes COBOL programs as they are defined and compiled on the target system where the program is intended to run, whether this is a mainframe or a PC. On the mainframe, the analyzer uses technology from CA-OPTIMIZER integrated with the COBOL compilers; on the PC, it integrates directly with the CA-Realia compiler. This approach ensures that what is being analyzed is exactly the program as it is seen by the compiler.

The results are downloaded to the workstation for visualization through an integrated gateway, based on the Common Communication Interface (CAICCI). The two platforms are connected only when programs are selected and downloaded from the mainframe library. Analysis can continue on the workstation without an expensive mainframe connection.

CA-COBOLVISION Program Analysis Functions

CA-COBOLVISION provides a visual framework for analysis of COBOL programs, presenting flow of control, data flow, data definitions, etc., in an interactive GUI environment. The GUI-based workstation cooperates with the program analysis and debugging components on mainframes and PCs, presenting developers with the same analysis environment regardless of where the program is compiled.

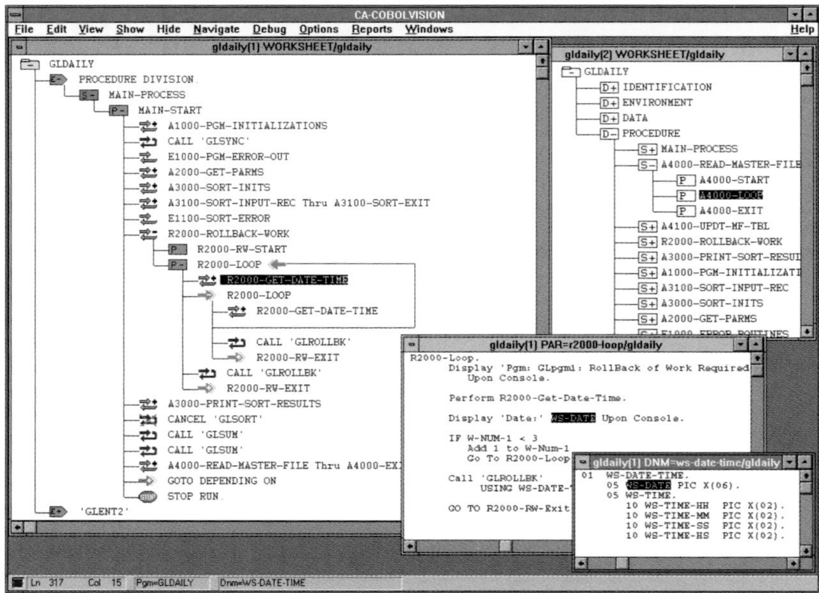

CA-COBOLVISION uses a graphical user interface to visualize the structure of a COBOL program that is analyzed on the host system where it is compiled, whether this is a mainframe or the same workstation.

The system provides powerful and flexible visualization features that make even the largest and most complex programs easier to comprehend. COBOL programs may be viewed in *text mode, tree mode* and *flow mode*. In each view mode, developers have extensive control over the format and contents of the program display.

The program visualizer exploits the "multiple document" paradigm to present related information. Several different views of a program may be presented in separate but synchronized windows. In all view modes, any referenced object—a perform-paragraph, a subprogram, a data definition—may be opened in a separate window by double-clicking on it. If the referenced object is a separate subprogram in a separate file, CA-COBOLVISION loads the file, downloading analysis results from the mainframe if necessary.

Structure diagrams, graphically annotated and colorized source code, a linked multiple-window design and an object-oriented user interface combine to produce a uniquely effective presentation of complex program structure. The natural relationships that make up a program's essence—references to data items, control flow, lexical context—are vividly displayed and may be directly manipulated. Navigation through a large program with complex structure is conveniently done in a natural way.

Viewing Flexibility

Text view mode displays the program in its original source format. Different types of statements may be selectively included, excluded or color coded: program structure, conditional statements, unreferenced data items, dead code, etc. Preprocessor code, copybooks, comments, etc., may be included or excluded from view.

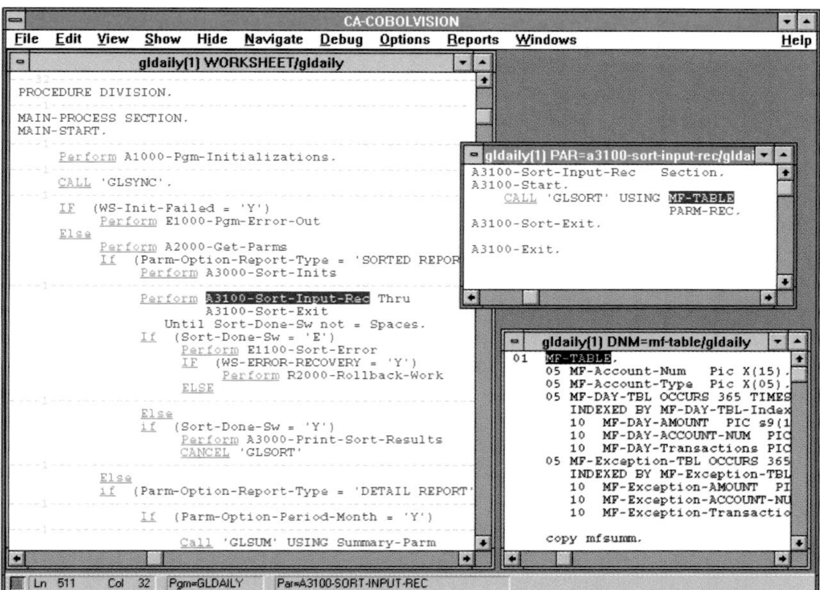

Text mode displays the original source code with optional color coding.

The text view also provides for navigation forward or backward along the logical path through the program. The developer can select the path to take at any branching point. For control statements, such as PERFORM and CALL, the system can optionally open the referenced paragraph in a separate window and continue navigating the path, as deeply as desired.

The example shown here illustrates the value of logical path analysis. Either this program was originally written with incorrect indentation, or the PERFORM THRU statement contains an unintended period. A maintenance programmer trying to understand the logic of the program may easily be misled by the indentation and miss the period, but the automatic analysis and visual presentation of CA-COBOLVISION helps avoid the mistake.

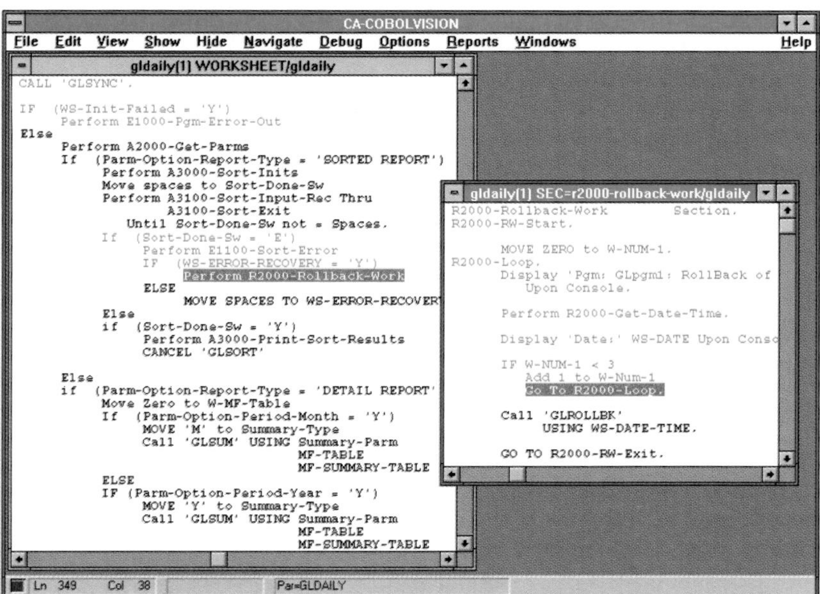

Path navigation displays the logical flow through the program.

Tree view mode displays the lexical structure of the program in a hierarchical outliner format, using a "table of contents" metaphor. Each branch of the tree represents a Division, Section, Paragraph, Group or Elementary data element definition. Individual branches may be expanded or collapsed. This mode provides an overview of the components of a program and a highly convenient method of navigating among them or selecting a component for further study (easily and immediately accomplished with the mouse).

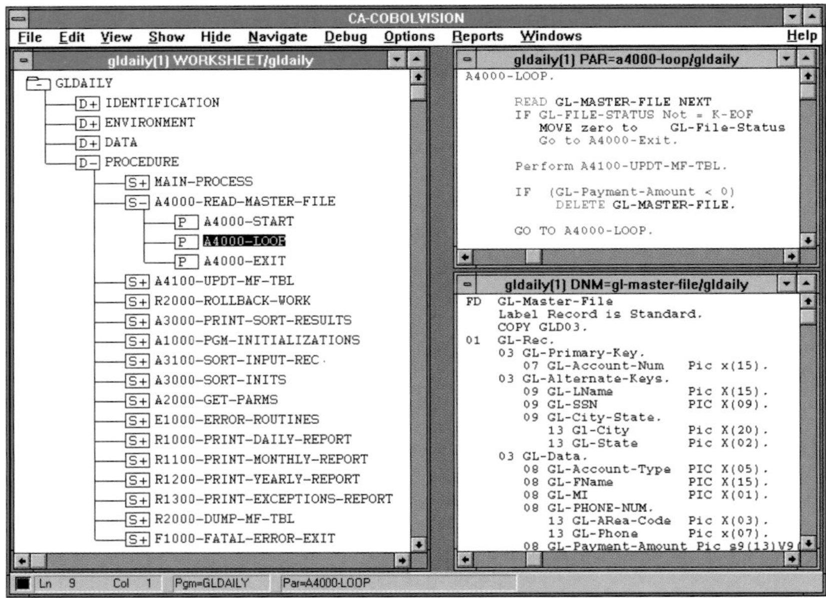

Tree mode displays the lexical structure of the program in an outliner ("table of contents") format.

Flow Diagram view mode graphically represents the control flow of the program by illustrating the relationships between various transfer verbs such as GO TO, PERFORM and CALL statements, and the programs, sections and paragraphs they reference. The extent of loops is graphically indicated. Each branch of the control flow may be expanded as deeply as desired. Note that unlike the static lexical program structure, depicted by the tree view, the flow diagram view depicts a dynamic runtime structure. Its branches are dynamic and may be expanded indefinitely. Again, any referenced component may be immediately opened in a window, even if it is in a different program.

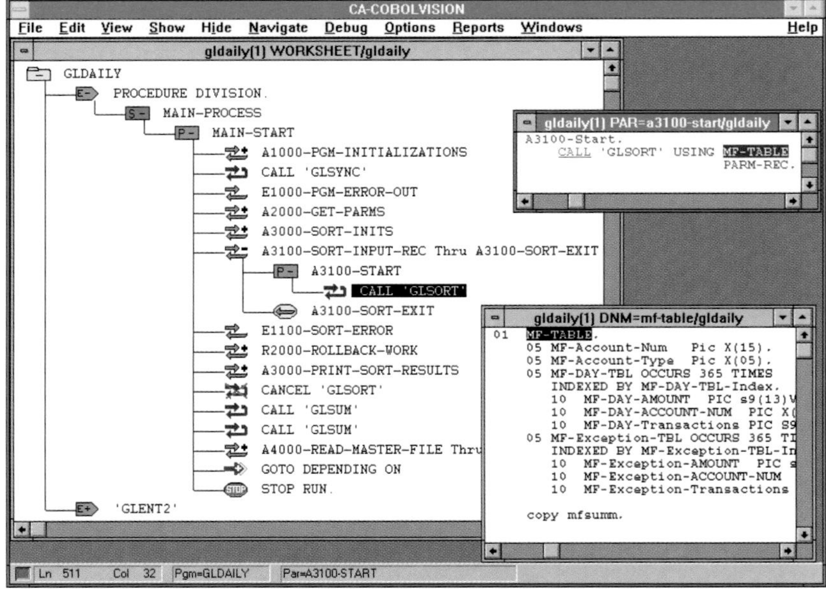

Flow Diagram mode graphically displays the control flow and invocation structure of the application. Referenced paragraphs and data items may be opened in separate windows.

Object-Oriented User Interface

Every identifiable entity within CA-COBOLVISION, a subprogram, paragraph, label or data name, is treated as an object that has its own special properties. Selecting an object and pressing the right mouse button invokes the "property inspector" which displays a menu of the different actions available for each type of object: jump to its definition, open the object definition in a separate window, find all references to it, etc.

The menu lists only those actions that are appropriate, given the type of the selected object and the context in which the object appears. For example, a quoted literal that follows the word CALL is correctly treated as a reference to a subprogram, while the same quoted literal in a DISPLAY statement is treated as a simple string.

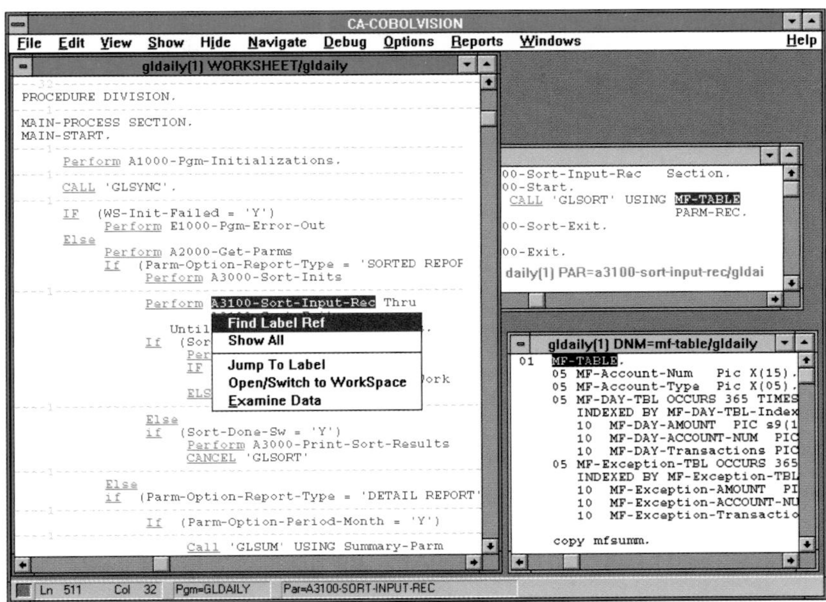

Property inspector presents a local menu with the options available for the selected entity: open it in a separate window, show references to it, etc.

Some actions may or may not be available depending on the capabilities of the current CA-COBOLVISION session. For example, the *definition* of a data item may always be displayed, but its *value* is available only when a debugging session is active. CA-COBOLVISION recognizes object types, context and session capabilities, adding a layer of common sense to the user interface.

Multitasked Analysis

The structure of the CA-COBOLVISION framework exploits the multitasked GUI environment to allow the developer to analyze several programs or program components simultaneously. Each program may be opened in several different windows, displaying different view modes or scrolled to different positions.

The integration of the analysis function with the development and debugging components further increases the value of this multitasked framework. A developer can download an additional program from a mainframe library, perform some mainframe-based debugging, compare its execution on the workstation version, and do some in-depth analysis of program structure and data interdependence, all within a single environment and without losing the thread of each session.

Visualization For GUI Restructuring

Although not usually considered maintenance, adapting an existing COBOL program to a GUI environment benefits from the same kind of analysis as standard maintenance. Unlike routine maintenance, which typically leaves the program structure intact but changes detail processing, "recycling" of programs into a GUI framework retains individual pieces of processing logic but modifies the overall structure.

This restructuring requires the identification of logically separate processing modules and the interdependencies (data and control) that exist among them. These independent modules can be packaged as "object handlers" or "event handlers" (see Chapter 14). This separation requires that the interdependency threads are implemented as shared data or control structures, either in a procedural or in an object-oriented framework.

As discussed in Section IV, the CA-Visual Objects architecture supports the use of standard code in legacy languages embedded within the object-oriented system, providing a home for the restructured code.

This technique of reengineering legacy applications is a tremendously powerful way of leveraging investments, and it benefits from exactly the same kind of analysis that CA-COBOLVISION provides for standard maintenance.

CHAPTER 10

Testing, Debugging And QA

Debugging has long been viewed as a difficult, yet necessary activity that requires a tremendous amount of patience and knowledge of the program and the language in which the program is written. This has traditionally meant that the most knowledgeable and experienced programmers are dedicated to the most difficult debugging tasks instead of developing new solutions. What is needed to counter this productivity drain are debugging tools that reduce the degree of program and language knowledge required.

CA Application Development Software provides the major tools used on a day-to-day basis in the testing, debugging and verification of mainframe-based legacy applications. Regression test systems, such as the mainframe-based CA-VERIFY and the workstation-based CA-TRAPS, help a development organization ensure that mission-critical applications remain fully functional after every change, whether perfective (adding functions), corrective (fixing bugs) or adaptive (adapting to changes in the environment). Mainframe-based debugging tools, such as CA-InterTest and CA-EZTEST, combined with the analysis tools of CA-OPTIMIZER and CA-OPTIMIZER II, have long provided the framework for identifying and solving the problems.

The next generation debugging system is a distributed analyzer/debugger, such as CA-COBOLVISION, which integrates the technology of these mainframe analysis and runtime debugging systems with a multitasking graphical front-end workstation. It is capable of supporting the more complex structures of applications in the new environment, including simultaneous debugging of two cooperative programs, even when they operate on different systems.

Distributed Testing And Debugging

Testing, debugging and QA present the same opportunity for distributed processing, and the same dilemma, as program analysis. A GUI-based desktop workstation offers many tempting benefits: not only the very clear and attractive graphical representation, invaluable for describing complex program structures, but more importantly the multitasking environment that allows developers to do debugging, inspect source code, and study any other relevant material, all at the same time.

On the other hand, while workstation development naturally includes workstation testing, the final test should be done on the target machine, whether this is a mainframe, midrange system, LAN or PC, because no emulation of a system is ever perfect.

GUI Workstation For Host-Based Testing

Cooperative processing, with the testing on the host and the user interface on the workstation, provides the best of both worlds. It ensures that the test is valid since it is performed on the target system in a real-world environment, yet gives the developer a user interface with all the power and flexibility the GUI approach can offer.

The same GUI environment is, of course, well-suited to workstation-based development testing. The distributed operating mode works equally well whether the test system is a remote mainframe or a different process on the same system. Even though the program being test-executed on the PC operates in 3270 mode, the GUI environment presents debugging and analysis information graphically.

CA-COBOLVISION Debugging Functions

The CA-COBOLVISION debugging component uses this distributed architecture for debugging as well as program analysis. The GUI environment furnishes a debugging session with separate windows for tracing the source code being executed, inspecting local variables and setting and managing breakpoints. The actual test execution of the COBOL program is done on the mainframe, viewed in a terminal emulator window, or on the PC using CA-Realia.

The mainframe test component uses technology from CA-InterTest, interacting with the desktop workstation while the test execution goes on; the CICS session is presented in a terminal emulation window, and the testing environment is shown in other windows. When running a test on the PC, CA-Realia COBOL provides a fully compatible environment for the program being tested, including CICS emulation; just as for mainframe testing, the tested program is shown executing in one window and the testing facilities in other windows.

The multitasking framework allows a developer to simultaneously debug several programs in different host environments. For example, a CICS transaction may be actively debugged through a connection to a mainframe while the same program is simultaneously run locally on the PC under CA-Realia. This means that it is now possible, for the first time, to *dynamically* compare the execution time behavior of a program operating in two very different environments. Data, execution flow and results can be compared to validate that a program is functionally equivalent in both worlds. This kind of multi-platform evaluation is invaluable for the difficult migration to multi-platform environments.

Synergy With Analyzer

The debugger component of CA-COBOLVISION is closely integrated with the analyzer component. This provides a number of synergistic benefits:

- Program source and structure analysis may be done simultaneously with the debugging, in different windows
- Program analysis may be used to guide the placement of breakpoints, through integration between the two functions
- Data items may be selected for runtime monitoring from the source text view using all the power of the analysis function
- Data values may be inspected side-by-side with the COBOL definition of the data item
- Tables are examined via subscripts that are restricted to valid ranges
- Numeric data is displayed in a format that is aware of the definition and takes into account human ergonomics

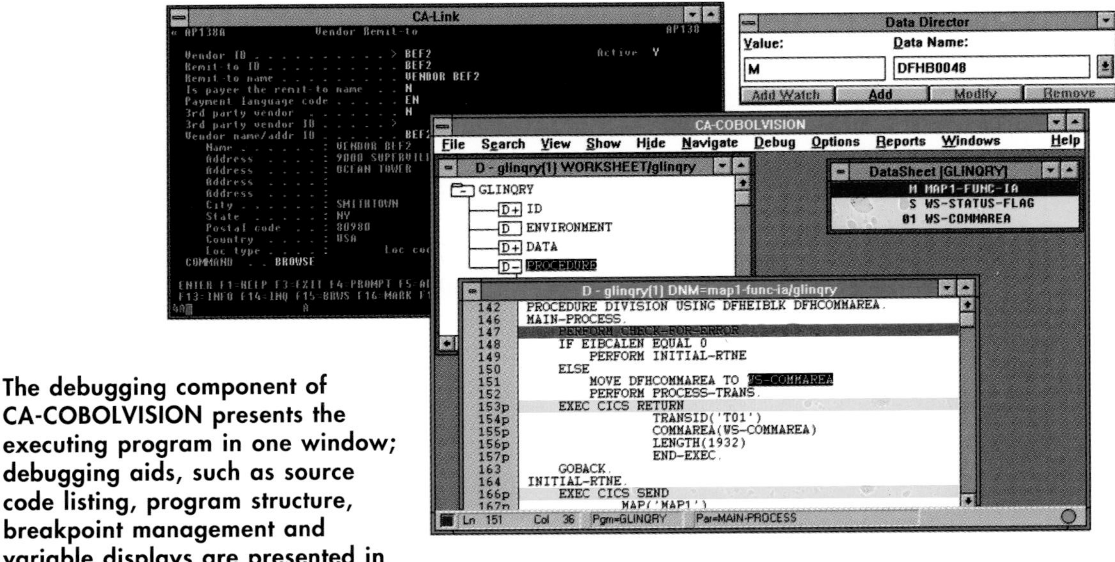

The debugging component of CA-COBOLVISION presents the executing program in one window; debugging aids, such as source code listing, program structure, breakpoint management and variable displays are presented in other windows. The debugging environment is identical whether the test program runs on the same workstation or on a mainframe under a cooperative processing framework.

Data Analysis

Most data analysis is handled through the Data Director, a modeless dialog box that provides for monitoring or editing the values of data items. The current values of a number of data items may be monitored in a Data Sheet, an independently movable and sizable window. Each program may have its own Data Sheet, continuously showing the values of local data items. Data items and their values are presented according to COBOL conventions, reflecting both the original program context and COBOL data types.

Data items may be selected for monitoring or editing by typing in the name or selecting a name from a drop-down list in the Data Director, or simply by selecting the data item in a program text view and dragging it into the Data Sheet or Data Director. Its current value is immediately displayed, and the item remains monitored in the Data Sheet until it is deleted or dragged out of the Data Sheet.

The Data Director also provides for setting a "watch" on a data item. This is a kind of breakpoint that is not associated with a specific line; instead, it halts program execution at whatever line changes the value. The breakpoint may be set to trigger after a certain number of changes.

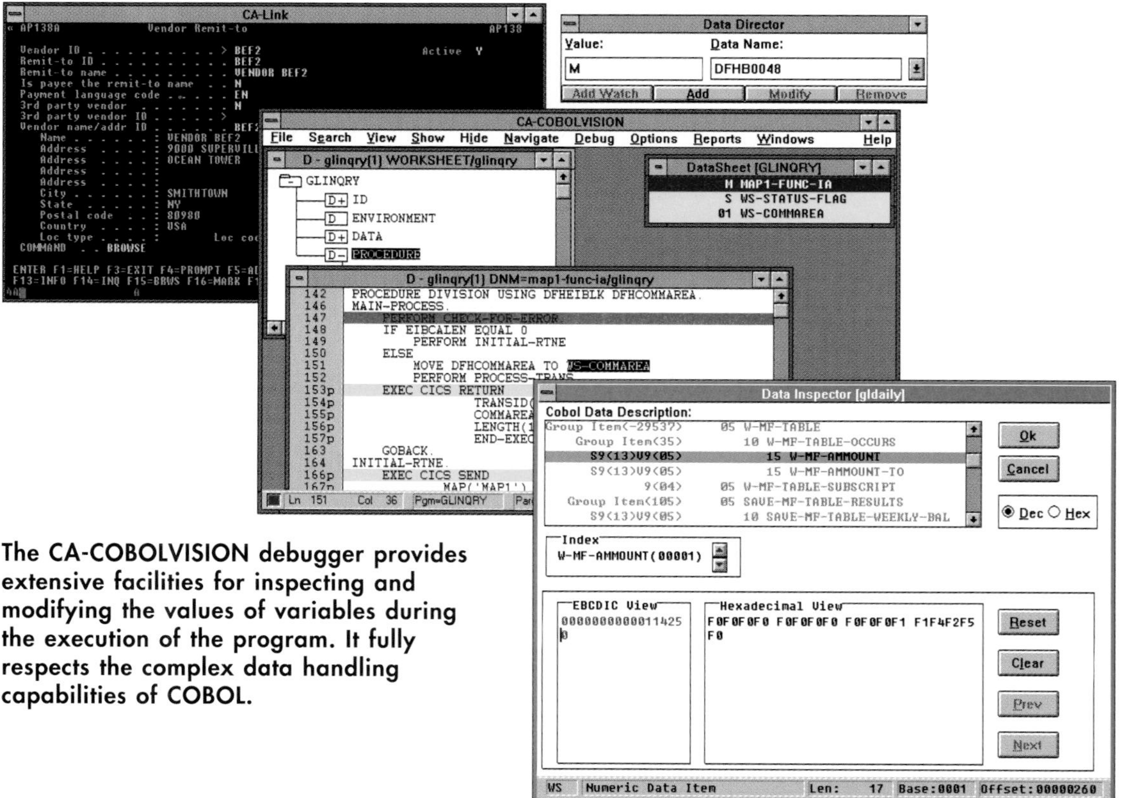

The CA-COBOLVISION debugger provides extensive facilities for inspecting and modifying the values of variables during the execution of the program. It fully respects the complex data handling capabilities of COBOL.

Breakpoint Management

Traditional debuggers do not have intrinsic knowledge of the program being debugged or the subtleties of the language in which it is coded. The CA-COBOLVISION debugger utilizes the knowledge base acquired by the analyzer component, and thereby automates many of the housekeeping tasks that are otherwise a burden. This is apparent in the various ways in which breakpoints may be set under CA-COBOLVISION:

- A line can have one or more conditional breakpoints assigned to it in addition to an unconditional breakpoint
- Conditions are constructed from list boxes that present only those comparisons that make sense; for example, a packed decimal field is not normally compared to an alphabetic field (except possibly using a hexadecimal literal comparison)
- Selecting a data item in a text view automatically fills in the left-hand side of a condition, allowing a developer to analyze a program and immediately construct a condition based on some interesting data item
- Breakpoint placement understands COBOL syntax: breakpoints may be placed only on executable lines; setting a breakpoint on a multiline statement does not require identifying the first line
- Breakpoints, conditional or unconditional, may be set automatically for sets of similar COBOL statements based on the type of verb that defines the statement; for example, all CALL statements may be selected at once

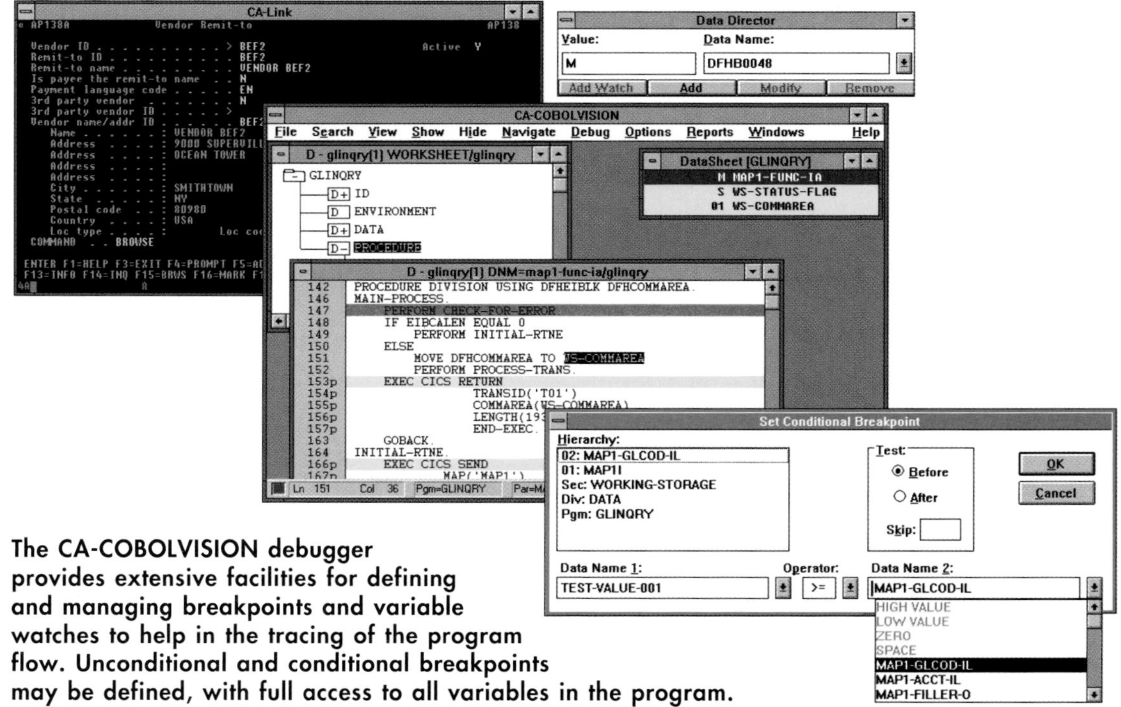

The CA-COBOLVISION debugger provides extensive facilities for defining and managing breakpoints and variable watches to help in the tracing of the program flow. Unconditional and conditional breakpoints may be defined, with full access to all variables in the program.

Breakpoints may be reviewed three different ways:

- By scrolling through the text view and individually examining each line that has a background color indicating a breakpoint
- By invoking the "Active Breakpoints" dialog which lists all breakpoints in one window and all conditions associated with each breakpoint in another
- By invoking the "Active Conditions" dialog which lists all conditions in one list box and all breakpoints associated with each condition in another list box

In the text view, the CA-COBOLVISION debugger color-codes statements to indicate the type or types of breakpoints that are set for a line:

- Red—indicates an unconditional breakpoint, a line at which the program will unconditionally stop
- Yellow—indicates a conditional breakpoint, a line at which execution will halt if a condition is met
- Orange—indicates there is an unconditional and one or more conditional breakpoints (red + yellow = orange)
- Magenta—indicates the current line at which execution has halted
- Green—indicates a temporarily disabled breakpoint

Debugger Integrated With Analyzer, Development Environment

While the CA-COBOLVISION debugger and analyzer are of significant value by themselves, and provide a major productivity breakthrough in development, maintenance and debugging of COBOL programs, even greater synergistic value is returned by the integration of these tools within the CA-Realia II development environment. By eliminating the hard barriers between different kinds of sessions, allowing the developer to have the same resources at all times, the overall productivity of the entire application life cycle is significantly improved.

SECTION IV

Applications For The New Environments

Construction Of Applications For The New Environments

Development of new applications for the new computing environments requires a new generation of tools. The power and flexibility of technologies such as graphical user interfaces and client/server architectures demand development systems oriented toward new application structures.

The high expectations on flexibility and responsiveness in the new business climate further raises the demands on application development. Traditional development paradigms cannot meet these demands. Today's and tomorrow's world requires an incremental development approach, a paradigm of stepwise refinement during the entire life of the application.

The CA-Visual Objects system is designed for an interactive, iterative development process, providing visual development tools integrated in an interactive visual workbench. These tools are built on a solid foundation of several key technologies: an object-oriented repository, object-oriented languages, an industrial-strength compiler supporting incremental compilation with entity-level granularity, client/server technology and an open database architecture.

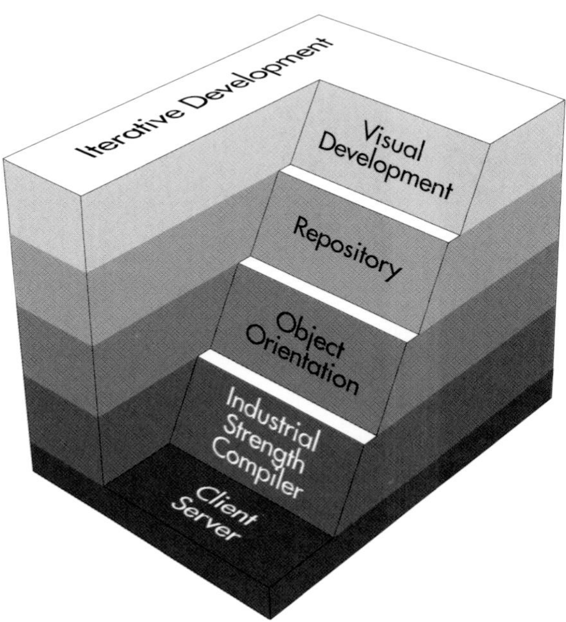

High-level visual tools for iterative development are built on a solid bedrock of a repository-based framework, object orientation, industrial-strength compiler technology and client/server architectures.

Each of these is valuable in itself, but the value increases synergistically when they are used together. Visual development is useful by itself, but is particularly effective when combined with object orientation. A development environment integrally based on a repository is highly effective, but especially so when it is based on an object-oriented architecture. Object orientation and graphical user interfacing are valuable, but without a robust compiler, their performance would be inadequate. Combined in this manner, the new technologies create not only a strong programming system, but a complete environment that not only addresses the technical challenges of computing in the 90s, but also improves the efficiency of the entire process.

These technologies are linked back to established languages and databases in a number of products, centered around the CA-Visual Objects architecture, that provide a new technology framework yet preserve language familiarity for experienced developers. The general-purpose compiler technology is imbued with language-specific flavors: the various Xbase dialects, third-generation languages and fourth-generation languages. The CA-Visual Objects system extends all the mainstream business languages: CA-Visual Objects for Clipper, dBFast, dBASE IV and FoxPro provide the growth path for Xbase developers; CA-Visual Objects for COBOL, IDEAL, ADS and TELON provide the growth path for mainframe developers.

For technical and system programming where the C and C++ languages dominate, the CA-C++ platform-independent compiler provides a robust multi-platform foundation, together with the CA-CommonView platform-adaptive GUI class library for C++.

CA-Visual Objects delivers these technologies for all the new platforms: Windows under DOS, PM under OS/2, Windows NT, and Motif under UNIX; other platforms may follow.

The new development systems exploit the established techniques for life cycle management, including networked library management and version control. They are based on an open database architecture that supports indexed file systems and the Xbase DBF database structure; relational client/server databases such as CA-DB, SQLServer, Oracle and other major third-party databases; and downsized, network versions of mainframe databases such as CA-IDMS and CA-DATACOM.

This section describes the CA-Visual Objects architecture from the foundation up. It first describes object orientation and its implementation in compiler and runtime support services. It goes on to the integrated visual workbench, first the repository and then the visual development tools. It then describes the client/server architecture with remote procedure call support and open database architecture. Finally, it describes the man–machine interface, including the graphical user interface services, the graphics and image-processing tools, and the reporting subsystem.

CHAPTER 11

Object Orientation

Far from being a new technology, object orientation was invented in Europe in the 1960s and first provided in a language called Simula 67. Praised by the cognoscenti, the language and the concept languished unrecognized outside the halls of academe. The development of object orientation was continued in languages such as Smalltalk, but it remained a niche technology (a delicate way of saying that it had little impact on the real world).

In recent years, object orientation has not only been revived but has been hailed as the cornerstone of software development for the new computer environments. Why the sudden shift? Should we give credence to this newfound enthusiasm, or is object orientation just another fad doomed to go the way of a long line of predecessors? If object orientation is the cornerstone of software development in the 90s, why wasn't it in the 70s or 80s?

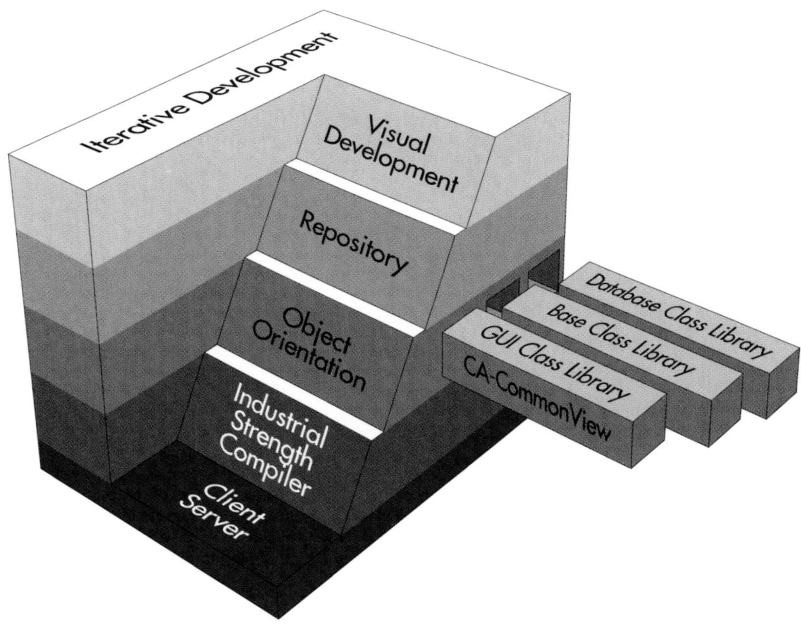

The object-oriented foundation technology is extended with class libraries that provide essential runtime services: graphical user interfacing, database interfacing, base classes for data management, etc.

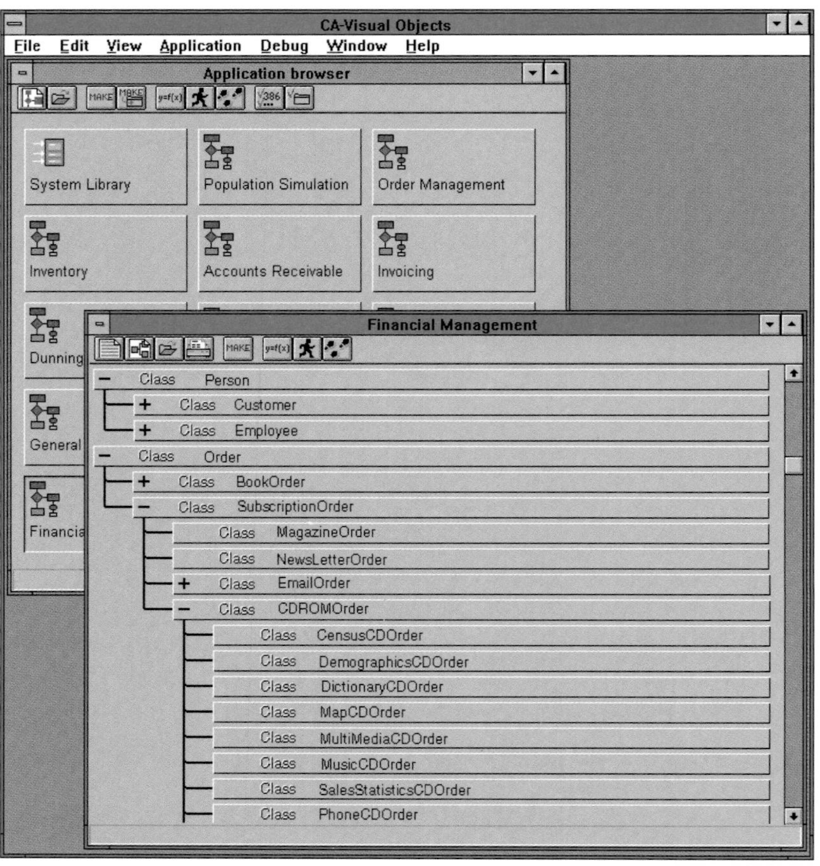

The class browser in CA-Visual Objects systems shows hierarchical class structure, an abstraction reflecting the real structure of the business world addressed by the application.

Object orientation is not an arcane academic theory prized for theoretical elegance. It is a pragmatic approach to managing complexity. As such, it is quite effective. And complexity is of course a very real concern, at the root of most IS challenges. The reason object orientation did not come to dominate the world is that, like any technique that promises productivity improvements after an initial training investment, it faced a credibility gap. It also faced competition from other techniques with similar goals, such as structured programming, 4GLs, code generators, artificial intelligence and CASE.

What brought object orientation to its current prominence is the complexity of building graphical user interfaces. Using standard procedural programming techniques for GUI programming is akin to using Assembler to build a business system: it is certainly possible, but it is neither easy nor efficient, only the elite do it well, and the resultant programs tend to be brittle and hard to maintain because there is little internal structure and no protection. Commercial Windows programs sometimes go through a 12 month beta test program with 10,000 testers—not a viable approach for in-house business application development.

New methods are needed if we are going to make GUI commonplace in commercial information processing. The object orientation paradigm is not only good at handling complexity in general, it is particularly well-suited to provide structure for the independently active windows, menus, tool boxes and dialog boxes of an event-driven GUI program. It was this specific need for GUI programming tools that made object orientation a household word among real-world programmers after years of languishing in obscurity.

Down-To-Earth Extensions Of Familiar Concepts

Behind the arcane jargon in which the industry is fond of shrouding its technology, the basic concepts of object orientation are quite down-to-earth and straightforward extensions of familiar business programming concepts:

A *class* extends the concept of a record or structure, a group of data elements accessed together, to include not only data but also the code to process that data. The code is provided in procedures called *methods*. The definition of a class is a form of type declaration; to use it you create one or more *objects* of that class.

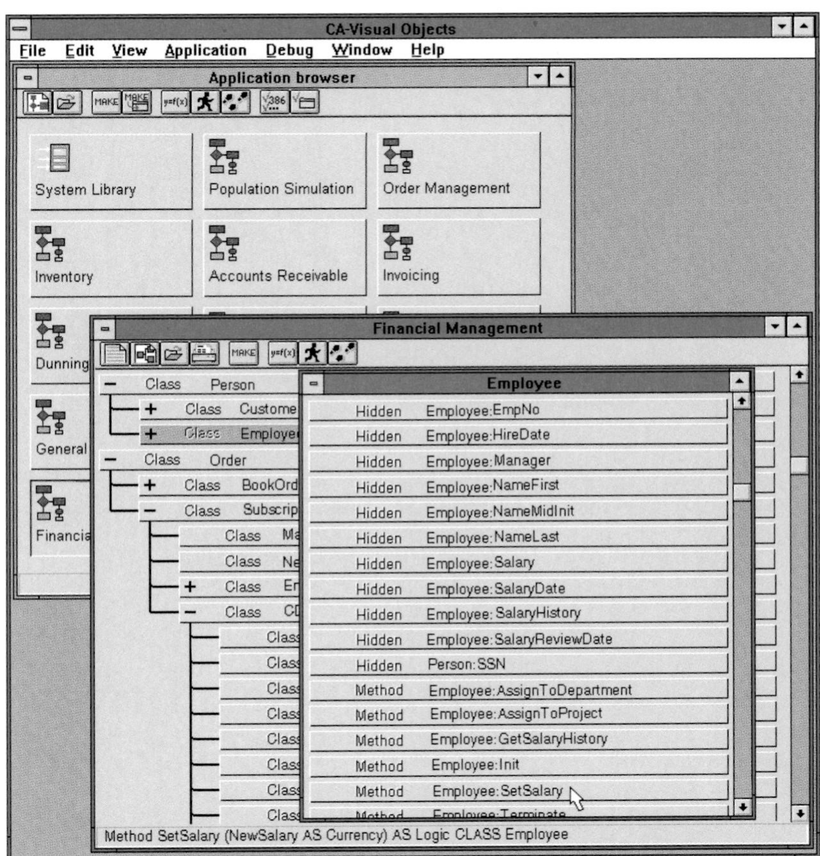

The "inspection window" of a class shows its components: hidden instance variables and methods, both its own and those inherited from its parent class, the Person. ("Methods" are procedures that act on objects such as persons and orders.)

Encapsulation (the time-honored principle of *information hiding*) means that only those characteristics of the class that are explicitly *exported* are accessible by other program elements; the rest are *hidden*. *Data elements* may be hidden or exported; the *definition* of methods—call sequence, formal parameters and return values—are exported, but their *implementations* are not.

Inheritance allows the definition of a class as a special case of another class, with the same attributes as the base class but with possible additions or modifications. For example, a Purchase Order contains some data elements such as the order number and some procedures such as SubmitToInvoicing; a RentalOrder *adds* attributes such as PaymentFrequency and *modifies* the SubmitToInvoicing procedure.

Polymorphism allows the program to deal with a set of Purchase Orders, executing the SubmitToInvoicing procedure for each and automatically getting the right version of the procedure depending on what kind of Purchase Order each object is.

What Is Object Orientation Really?

There is a great deal of confusion in the industry about the term "object orientation," which is sometimes used as marketing hype without any specific meaning. In particular, many purportedly object-oriented systems allow the creation of objects of existing classes, but not the definition of new classes. In accordance with accepted industry practice, we use the term precisely, requiring that a system support the four key technologies to qualify as object-oriented: class definition and instantiation, encapsulation, inheritance and polymorphism.

Systems that support some but not all of these functions are properly termed "object-based." For example, it is common to borrow some but not all of the concepts and syntax of object orientation when adding GUI support to a language. For example, CA-dBFast, CA-Clipper 5.0 and CA-REALIZER are all object-based. CA-Clipper is extended to full object orientation under DOS, and of course the growth path for both CA-Clipper and CA-dBFast leads to the fully object-oriented CA-Visual Objects system.

Key Object Orientation Concepts

Object

An entity that contains both attributes (data, such as a COBOL record) and behavior (procedures associated with the object). The procedures are commonly called methods; invoking a procedure is called "sending a message to the object."

Class

A data type declaration: a category of objects with the same attributes and behaviors, for example "purchase order."

Instantiation

Creating an object, or an instance of a class, for example "purchase order 123456."

Encapsulation

The isolation of attributes and behaviors from surrounding layers and structure. The "purchase order" class may keep a linked list of its line items, but the details of its implementation are not known to any other object or procedure, only the ability to retrieve each line item for processing.

Abstraction

The decomposition of a problem into its component levels. The most abstract level describes the components in their most general sense. A general "purchase order" is abstract, a "subscription order" is a more concrete case of a purchase order, a "weekly magazine subscription order" is even more concrete.

Subclassing

The definition of a class hierarchy by defining a class as a (more concrete) special case of some more general class. A subscription order is a subclass of a purchase order.

Inheritance

The mechanism for sharing attributes and behaviors among layers of a class hierarchy. Behaviors defined at higher (more abstract) levels of the hierarchy can be accessed or redefined at a lower (more concrete) level. For example, a subscription order automatically has an order number and a customer ID like any other purchase order.

Polymorphism

The ability to send the same message to different objects and achieve the appropriate result. You might execute the "Invoice" command for different purchase orders and get the expected, but somewhat different, action from each.

Code Reuse

Once it was accepted as a tool for GUI programming, the overriding strength of object orientation was recognized: it facilitates reusability of code, long recognized as the most powerful method of improving development productivity. Indeed, code reuse is the only economy of scale available in software engineering. No technique for constructing a program is as efficient as not having to do it at all.

Because a *class* or an *object* is complete, and contains both the data definition and the code to process it, it simplifies the management of reused code when its author is not available for consultation.

Encapsulation formalizes the difference between the fixed, externally published characteristics of an object and the possibly fluid internal implementation details. Other code cannot become dependent on hidden implementation details, and therefore change propagation is reduced.

Inheritance provides a safe, formal method of modifying reused code. With traditional techniques, the only way to change a piece of code that is not exactly right is to modify the source code, with negative implications on reliability, change propagation and version management.

Polymorphism allows existing code designed for operating on a base object to continue operating on its modified variants. Just as an object-oriented GUI system can provide platform-adaptive behavior, so can an object-oriented business solution be adaptive to changes consistent with the overall framework of the business abstraction.

Technical And System Programming

The most popular object-oriented system today is C++. It owes its popularity to four main factors. It is a fully compatible superset of C, which is the most popular language for technical and system programming on non-mainframe systems. It extends C with a number of powerful technologies, including object orientation, in a clean way that lets the developer choose which object-oriented features to use. In general, it supports programming better than any competitive language (indeed, it is hard to identify a credible competitor). And, perhaps most important, it preserves the efficiency and economy of C.

These characteristics make C++ the preferred language for writing technical and system software, such as compilers, operating systems, graphics systems, etc. C++ is not designed for business development, and lacks a number of important features that are required in business applications, including such ordinary functions as formatting of dollar values or validating data entry.

Because of its system programming heritage, C++ is fairly bristling with features. This richness makes the language difficult to learn, and makes its use difficult to manage and control. C++ applications are often difficult to understand and therefore difficult to maintain.

Advanced compiler and repository technology can help alleviate this last problem. Development is under way to extend the CA-C++ compiler and development system to provide more application-wide and enterprise-wide checking, not only of technical correctness, but of idiomatic use of the language.

Complete Object-Oriented Systems

C++ follows the philosophy of C: it extends C, but does not change the basic paradigm of the language. Like C, C++ is a lean and mean and extremely efficient language that adds no overhead for the convenience of the developer. It explicitly leaves major responsibilities to the programmer, in particular the entire area of memory management. This allows the developer to optimize an application, but also makes the language very demanding. Any mistake in this fundamental area can have far-reaching consequences, ranging from complete system crashes to the insidious "memory creep" that afflicts so many Windows programs (they gradually gum up the works—after a period of use, the system must be restarted to clean out debris still allocated in memory).

Because memory and pointer management in an object-oriented system is fundamental to its operation and quite complex, most classical object-oriented systems have provided a "garbage collection" scheme which automatically finds and discards objects that are no longer used. Combined with automatic allocation of memory and implicit handling of pointers, such systems insulate the developer from the technical complications of the object-oriented system.

Automating the facilities of object orientation is not only useful, it is very nearly necessary to allow object orientation to become a part of mainstream IS. However, it is possible to go too far in the direction of "object orientation purity." Many purely object-oriented systems make everything an object, even ordinary integer variables. While this makes for a clean and simple environment—an integer may be subclassed just like a Purchase Order—the performance implications are serious. Where a compiled classical language can use one machine instruction to retrieve a value, a completely object-oriented system must follow pointers, do table lookups and resolve a lot of ambiguities just to find the value and even more to operate on it. "Hybrid" object-oriented languages such as C++ retain the efficiency of standard languages for standard operations on standard data, while providing all the convenience and power of object orientation where desirable.

Thus, on the one hand we have C++, which sacrifices convenience for the sake of efficiency; on the other we have purist object-oriented systems that sacrifice efficiency for the sake of convenience. Is it possible to design a system to have the best of both worlds?

It is. CA-Visual Objects is a hybrid language. Like C++, it compiles standard operations on standard data to the same machine instructions as standard languages such as C or COBOL. Its object orientation, however, provides automatic memory allocation, automatic handling of pointers including de-referencing, and automatic garbage collection. The developer can use object orientation for big important things without having to worry about the efficiency of adding two numbers.

Object Orientation In Business Languages

One of the main barriers to acceptance of object orientation has been that it is not provided in common languages. Business programmers do not use Smalltalk or Simula. If they come from the PC world, they use the Xbase family of languages (dBASE III and IV, CA-Clipper, CA-dBFast, FoxPro and others). If they come from mainframes, they use COBOL, CA-ADS, CA-IDEAL and CA-TELON.

C++ has been accepted as an object-oriented extension of a familiar language, C. Similarly, business programmers need object orientation integrated with Xbase, COBOL, CA-ADS, CA-IDEAL and CA-TELON. The CA-Visual Objects architecture provides this extension combined with language familiarity. CA-Clipper provides object-oriented extensions in a character-based mode.

Class Libraries

In an object-oriented system, supporting services are provided in the form of class libraries. The class libraries provide an elegant and extensible way of using these services. They integrate with the programming language and the development environment: class browsers and other repository facilities fully recognize and document the class library structure. Class libraries also provide an effective way of insulating application code from platform-specific implementation details.

The key class libraries of the CA-Visual Objects architecture are:

- Base classes that provide fundamental storage management utilities such as sets, stacks, lists and other useful services.
- Database classes that provide a higher level of abstraction than the underlying database operations. The database classes provide fundamental behavior common across different database implementations.
- The GUI class library, CA-CommonView, provides higher level functions in a platform-independent design and with platform-adaptive behavior. CA-CommonView is extended with high-level functions such as rich text handling and high-level controls such as the CUA '91 notebook.
- Graphics for charting of data, on-screen and on hard copy.
- Image processing for storage, display and printing of images, including full-color, photographic quality images.
- A reporting class library that allows an application to execute predefined CA-RET reports, under the control of runtime parameters for data retrieval and report appearance. The report can execute as a separate task with automatic queuing.
- Error handling.
- Intertask communication through clipboard, DDE and OLE.

Internally, the class libraries are implemented in different ways: as purely object-oriented CA-Visual Objects code (the base classes), as an object-oriented interface to procedural C or COBOL code (graphics, image processing), as a "thin" CA-Visual Objects interface layer to object-oriented C++ code (the "Cheshire cat" architecture used with CA-CommonView), or as an interface to an external process (reporting).

When used within C++, the class libraries can provide much of the automation missing in the base C++ "tool kit" system. CA-CommonView, for example, automates much of the complex memory management required in GUI programming.

The GUI support architecture, graphics, image processing and reporting are described in Chapter 16.

Publication Of Business Solutions As Class Libraries

Object orientation is a powerful technique for coding, publishing and reusing code for the buttons, windows and dialog boxes of a GUI. It is an equally powerful technique for coding, publishing and reusing business code. Indeed, it can be expected that class libraries will become a common method for publishing applications.

With traditional software architectures, there is a strong differentiation in principle between vendors of business solutions, such as Accounts Payable and Accounts Receivable systems, and vendors of application development systems such as 4GLs. In practice, many clients need to customize the business applications, modifying or extending their functionality. For this reason, many business applications (including many from CA) are delivered with source code and development utilities. However, modifying a vendor's source code causes many problems: at the very least, difficulty in accepting upgrades to the product; in the worst case, stability problems and difficulty in getting support.

Because object orientation provides such a powerful and yet controlled and manageable way of customizing software, it is a safe way of delivering a product. The client can modify the application, by subclassing the standard business classes and extending or overriding its behavior, or by adding new functions that use the standard classes—without mixing up the source code and rendering it unmaintainable or unsupportable.

This evolution is likely to gradually eliminate the distinction between application and tool vendors, a distinction that is already tenuous today with so many applications including development tools.

CHAPTER 12

Compiler Technology

Interpretive languages such as BASIC and Xbase traditionally allow fully dynamic, undeclared, untyped, unscoped variables, with "late" (runtime) binding of operations to data. A programmer can write:

a **= 5**

without worrying about declaring ***a*** or defining its type (integer, short integer, floating point, etc.), scope (global over the whole application, local to the function or procedure, etc.) or allocation (dynamic or static). This is very convenient—it allows developers to see results quickly without worrying about technical details. Informal, dynamic data handling is one of the chief advantages of high-level languages such as Xbase, and is one of the keys to iterative development.

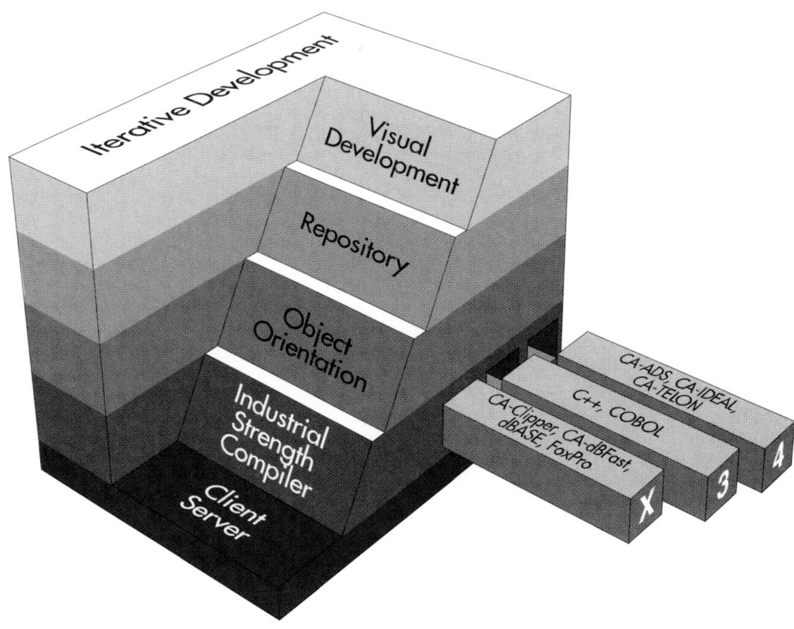

Language customization gives the CA-Visual Objects compiler the specific flavor for Xbase languages such as CA-Clipper, CA-dBFast, dBASE and FoxPro, third-generation languages such as C++ and COBOL, and mainframe-based fourth-generation languages and application generators such as CA-ADS, CA-IDEAL and CA-TELON. The object-oriented application structure and compiler optimization remains common across languages, but process code may be written in a language familiar to the developer.

But this freedom comes at a price. Languages such as C and COBOL, which require more rigor and formality in variable definition, offer several real-world benefits such as improved reliability, performance and development productivity in large projects. These benefits derive from "early" (compile-time) binding of operations to data. Late-bound, interpretive languages generally do not meet performance requirements for production applications, because each reference to a variable involves finding out *at runtime* what kind of information the variable contains at the moment. Languages that allow this informality are usually implemented as interpreters or "p-code compilers" (preprocessed interpreters). Early-bound, native mode compilers such as CA-Visual Objects and CA-Realia perform from 10 to 100 times faster than interpretive systems.

Optimization Of Data Management

When a program contains variables of specific type, scope and life, the compiler can produce tight and efficient code. For example, statements such as:

```
Local x,y as int
...
x := y
```

produce a direct assignment statement, usually a single machine instruction, with no extraneous memory management, conversion or runtime checking.

In contrast, working with variables of indeterminate type, statements such as:

```
// No declaration!
...
x := y
```

require a lot of code to allocate, free and reallocate the memory since there is no way of knowing, at compile time, what some distant procedure may have stored in **y** and hence what kind of conversion and memory allocation is required.

By allowing dynamic, globally scoped and untyped variables, most Xbase compilers (and of course all Xbase interpreters) are forced to produce very inefficient code. Because of the need for runtime handling of type translation and memory management, even compilers that produce "EXE" files actually produce "p-code" which is interpreted at runtime (this includes CA-Clipper, which is the most efficient Xbase compiler on the market).

How can a compiler produce optimal code for clean programs that use strongly typed variables, while at the same time allowing the loose untyped approach? We do not want to force the developer to switch over to an entirely clean approach, yet we want to optimize those statements and those variables that are optimizable while supporting all others.

With the question stated that way, the answer is obvious. The CA-Visual Objects compiler produces tight, fully optimized native machine code for all statements that use well-defined, fully declared variables, and intersperses p-code for statements that reference untyped variables.

In many cases, the CA-Visual Objects compiler can produce fully typed code even for untyped variables. A *data type inference* step can often determine the data type of a variable without explicit type declaration by analyzing the process flow of the code.

This approach *rewards* developers for producing more explicit code, but does not *require* a wholesale shift to a different way of programming. Indeed, by optimizing each individual statement and each individual variable, it rewards incremental improvement of the code. As individual functions and procedures of an application are cleaned up, they become more efficient; within a single function or procedure, individual statements become more efficient as each variable is defined more tightly.

The result is a compiler that is compatible with the traditional Xbase approach and supports the informality desired in prototyping while at the same time producing native compiled code as efficient as C or COBOL.

Strictly typed applications can also be more reliable because the declaration of a data type allows the compiler to check that the code is correct: an accidental assignment of *"hello"* to a variable declared as *integer* is detected during compilation and is prevented from causing problems during execution.

Specific scoping also improves reliability: by limiting access of a variable to a specific area, we reduce the risk of one function or procedure accidentally stepping on the data of another. It improves developer productivity by enabling reusability of code. Unless its data can be kept private, a function or procedure cannot reliably be reused in another application because of the risk of conflict of variable or function names. Specific scoping can improve performance significantly, because the compiler can produce tighter code without all the lookup, memory management, type translation and checking required at runtime to handle fully dynamic data.

What's a language designer to do? Provide the performance and integrity benefits of strict data definition or the convenience of the more lax regimen?

Optimization And Permissiveness

CA-Visual Objects illustrates the optimal solution: it allows but does not require programmers to

Data Typing And Scoping In CA-Visual Objects

By using the extended variable declaration facilities of CA-Visual Objects, developers can gain the precision, control and efficiency afforded by early binding in rigorous languages such as C and COBOL. To support the conventions of Xbase and the convenience of late binding as used in higher level languages and prototyping systems, undeclared variables are also allowed and are given conventional scoping, allocation and type conversions.

The ***lookup style, scope*** and ***allocation*** of variables can be:

Public Globally visible; dynamically allocated and untyped.

Private Visible in the function or procedure that owns it and any function called by it; dynamically allocated and untyped.

Global Visible over the entire application or a module (a region of the application); can be statically allocated and strongly typed.

Local Visible only in the function, procedure or method that owns it; can be statically allocated and strongly typed.

The **Static** modifier may be used to control the lifetime of locals and the visibility of globals, functions, classes, data types, etc.

The default scope for a variable with undefined scope is public if used in the main procedure, and private if used in a function or method, in accordance with Xbase convention.

The ***type*** of a variable can be:

- Undefined and dynamic
- Fixed to a predefined type
- Fixed to a user-defined type
- Any type of object
- Fixed to a specific class and its subclasses

The default type of an undeclared variable is dynamic unless the compiler's automatic type inferencing scheme can determine a type from the use of the variable. This scheme optimizes access to undeclared variables only, and may be explicitly disabled for individual variables.

define variables strictly, allowing (but not requiring) strict typing, scoping and memory management control. In the same way, CA-Clipper is the first Xbase compiler to allow lexical scoping. The compilers take advantage of all information the developer provides to optimize the generated code and verify the integrity of the code. CA-Visual Objects supports all forms of variable declaration provided in strongly typed and scoped languages, and fully exploits the information available for compile-time checking, static memory management and code generation without runtime data conversion.

By remaining fully compatible with the traditional unspecific Xbase programming style, the CA-Visual Objects compiler combines the benefits of both worlds: the quick and casual development so prized in prototyping and in development of smaller applications, and the formality and rigor required for development of mission-critical applications.

In many cases, the CA-Visual Objects compiler can determine the data type of a variable from context. This automatic type inferencing facility allows the compiler to optimize access even for less rigorously written code.

Optimization And Object Orientation Purity

Some object orientation purists argue that all elements of a class ("instance variables") should be hidden, and all access to the data should go through methods. This permits the class designer to change all aspects of its implementation without impacting users of the class. For example, instead of explicitly storing product prices in different currencies, an application could change its implementation to store a single price in dollars or yen and calculate other currencies upon demand. The "access" and "assign" methods insulate the rest of the application from this implementation change in the class, which appears unchanged externally.

However, a method invocation involves significantly more overhead than a direct access to a memory position, so pragmatically oriented developers demand the ability to access instance variables directly, without any intermediary processing. This is particularly important for objects that belong to a class hierarchy. Since methods may be redefined at any level in the hierarchy, the system must determine at runtime which version of the function should be executed for each object. This involves table lookup and late binding of both input parameters and return values.

CA-Visual Objects provides three types of handling of instance variables:

- HIDDEN—no direct access from outside the object; ACCESS and ASSIGN methods are allowed to provide external access, with late binding
- EXPORTED—direct access allowed from outside the object; early-bound; no ACCESS or ASSIGN methods
- PROTECTED—no direct access from outside the object; early-bound access from methods inside the object; no ACCESS or ASSIGN methods

This design allows a class designer to stick to purist principles for their undeniable advantages, or knowingly and carefully optimize performance with some sacrifice in maintainability. This is the kind of trade-off familiar to all software engineers; indeed, engineering has been defined as "the art of optimizing under constraints." Rather than argue over philosophical principles, engineers must provide the tools to control and manage these trade-offs.

Application-Wide Integrity Checking

The compiler, linker and automatic make facility automatically check the integrity of internal relationships in the application. They verify that entities such as functions, variables, constants, objects and methods are used correctly (in a technical sense), automatically verifying the data type of parameters and returned values (and inserting translation if necessary), and warning of unresolvable mismatches between call-by-value and call-by-reference in the calling and called entities. Note that many mismatches that would cause fatal errors in traditional languages are resolved here: missing parameters and polymorphic data are permitted unless explicitly excluded by the programmer.

Note that this validation is automatic, and does not require manual creation and management of header files or make files. The system automatically extracts the information it needs from the compilation.

Because the compiler and the entire development system are closely integrated with the repository (Chapter 13), integrity checking can be global and application-wide. The compiler has knowledge of all components of the application and can verify the consistency of all entity references *at compile time*. Indeed, since the repository extends across several applications, the system can verify the integrity of use of objects and functions shared between applications.

This integrity checking goes beyond that provided by theoretical design and analysis tools such as front-end CASE systems. Because the repository is actively integrated with the development system, it provides active verification during the entire development life cycle.

Data Types

The data types used in business languages such as COBOL and Xbase are very different from those used in languages aimed at system programming such as C. Business languages need to provide data types for handling currency with high degrees of precision, typically fixed decimal types, but have less need for pointers and other system programming types.

However, in order to allow interfacing with support libraries written in C, including the operating system and GUI support libraries, even business languages need to support the technical C data types. Some of these, such as pointers and window handles, do not fit well with business languages, but they must nonetheless be supported.

In an era when multiple platform support is a major consideration even for business programming, the languages must recognize the different data representations on different platforms. For example, both C and CA-Visual Objects provide two different sets of numeric types, one defined precisely as 16-bit, 32-bit and 64-bit on every platform, another defined more generally as "low precision," "standard precision" or "high precision" with platform-specific definitions.

CA-Visual Objects also supports both static (fixed size) and dynamic (variable size) arrays and strings, automatically allocating and deallocating the memory required.

In the new environments, applications will increasingly need to support "unstructured data" such as scanned documents, photographic images and fully formatted text. In addition to the support facilities in the graphics class libraries (see Chapter 16) and the database, the compiler also needs support for images, rich text and general-purpose, uninterpreted "BLOBs" (Binary Large Objects). The compiler and runtime system need to understand these data types and provide automatic memory management for them. Some of these new data types are implemented as native data types in the language, some as classes.

Compiler Efficiency

Native Compiler For Execution Speed

Performance and integrity have always been important issues for mission-critical applications, of course, but they are particularly critical during the transition to object-oriented, GUI-based, client/server architectures. These technologies are resource intensive, and unless the foundation implementation is strong enough, the end result will be unacceptable. Many approaches to improved development productivity have failed because they could not produce industrial-strength applications. Object orientation must be based on robust compiler technology.

Compilers are more efficient than interpreters. This commonly accepted fact remains valid, although the picture is confused somewhat by different flavors of compilers and interpreters.

Even CA-Clipper, the fastest Xbase compiler available, falls short of languages such as COBOL and C in terms of raw execution speed. This is because Xbase compilers do not fully compile the program to native machine code. They preprocess the program, digesting it into "p-code" which is executed by a runtime interpreter.

Performance Benchmarks

The core performance of the CA-Visual Objects compiler and its runtime facilities can be gauged from standard test programs that execute basic operations such as arithmetic and string manipulation and control structures such as looping and function calls. The standard "Sieve of Eratosthenes," which finds prime numbers, is an accepted benchmark for this kind of performance. In a recent test, the execution times were (in seconds):

- dBASE IV 1.1 — 1,030
- FoxPro — 409
- CA-Clipper Summer '87 — 540
- CA-Clipper 5.0 — 175
- CA-Visual Objects — 3
- C — 2

(Note: C and CA-Visual Objects ran under Windows while the others ran under DOS.)

Although appearing remarkable, the results are readily explained: dBASE IV is an interpreter; FoxPro and CA-Clipper Summer '87 are "p-code compilers," twice as fast; CA-Clipper 5.0 shows the benefits of explicit scoping, and is six times as fast; C and CA-Visual Objects are "real" compilers with explicit variable declaration and native code generation, several hundred times faster.

These results indicate the performance of the compiler or interpreter itself, and do not translate directly into application speed which includes database management and screen display. They nonetheless indicate the inherent robustness of the foundation provided by the CA-Visual Objects compiler, robustness that permits the addition of sophisticated but expensive facilities such as object orientation and graphical user interfaces.

There are several reasons why Xbase compilers work like this, but the main reason is the loose data specification of Xbase. In contrast, the stricter data specification facilities of CA-Visual Objects allow the compiler to produce native machine code as efficient as that produced by C and COBOL compilers.

Because CA-Visual Objects continues to permit undeclared, unspecified, dynamic variables, it must sometimes fall back on p-code to handle variables which can contain data of unknown type. This involves runtime testing and data conversion, but the performance overhead is restricted to those statements that involve unspecified variables. All statements within a function or procedure that are compilable are compiled to native machine code.

The developer is not required to write clean code, but is rewarded for doing so. The results are illustrated by the benchmark results shown above: execution speeds two orders of magnitude faster than the fastest Xbase compilers in existence.

Incremental Compiler For Compilation Speed

The productivity (and the happiness!) of a developer is highly dependent on the speed of compilation and linking. One of the fundamental reasons why PC development is so efficient is the ability to fix problems and try different approaches quickly. A responsive environment supports modern development techniques such as iterative development and prototyping.

The ability to immediately test a modified application without recompiling and relinking is one of the advantages commonly advocated for interpretive systems. Some developers accept slow execution as the price to pay for immediate test turn-around. Others use an interpretive environment for prototyping and switch to a compiler for producing the final application. This hybrid approach of course raises the possibility that the interpreter used for prototyping does not behave like the compiler; in many cases, the application must be debugged all over again, and often changed in material ways.

Again, it is possible to get the best of both worlds. Through a combination of fast compilation and a highly selective "make" facility, the CA-Visual Objects incremental compiler provides a responsive environment without requiring an interpreter.

The rapid response of the incremental compiler is based on its *entity-level granularity*, in contrast to the file-level granularity of conventional development systems. All "make" facilities rebuild an application after a change by finding all components that are affected, directly or indirectly, by the change and doing whatever recompilation, rebinding and relinking is necessary. With traditional development techniques, including C and COBOL, the impact analysis is done with a fairly coarse "granularity": if a source file has been changed or is affected by a change to another file, the entire source file must be recompiled.

CA-Visual Objects provides "object-level" or "method-level" granularity. If you modify a statement in an object method (a function), usually only that method requires recompilation; if you redefine a global variable, only the functions that directly access that variable require recompilation; if you modify a dialog box or a menu, only the resource file requires recompilation. Because CA-Visual Objects is inherently based on object-oriented principles, the make facility can be more selective than is possible in either C or C++ (or of course in traditional Xbase or COBOL).

Combined with a highly efficient compiler, this produces an environment where the developer can test the results of a local change in a few seconds or less, even in a large application with several thousand lines of code. Edit a function, a dialog box or a menu, click on the "Run" button, and see the changed program virtually instantaneously. An application that takes a few hours to recompile entirely, and 10 to 30 minutes to rebuild with a conventional "make" facility, may take a few seconds to rebuild with the CA-Visual Objects incremental compiler, depending on how pervasive the changes are. This responsiveness is envied by C developers as well as Xbase developers who have seen it.

This highly responsive development environment eliminates one of the reasons for having an interpretive system for prototyping. CA-Visual Objects combines the ideal environment for prototyping and trial-and-error development with the execution efficiency of an industrial-strength compiler.

CHAPTER 13

Repository-Based Development Environment

The Integrated Development Environment of the CA-Visual Objects architecture is designed to provide a productive framework for development of all kinds of applications. It ensures the integrity of mission-critical applications by providing organized management of all application components. It also provides powerful support for the iterative development paradigm by providing automatic search and browse facilities and immediate turn-around.

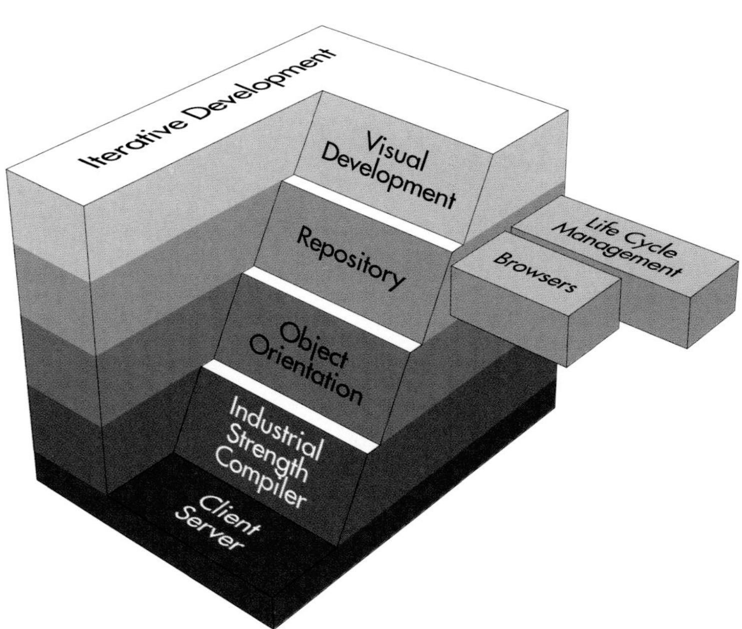

An object-oriented repository with browsers and integrated life cycle management forms the basis for the Integrated Development Environment.

The IDE is integrally based on an object-oriented repository. All aspects of working with application components, looking at them, analyzing their relationships and editing them, is done from the repository.

The CA-Visual Objects development environment does not normally use external program files, although it does of course support them. Every component of an application is stored in the repository. Finding, editing, compiling and debugging of application components is done without ever dealing directly with external files. The IDE presents component browsers and editors in subwindows under an MDI (Multiple Document Interface) paradigm.

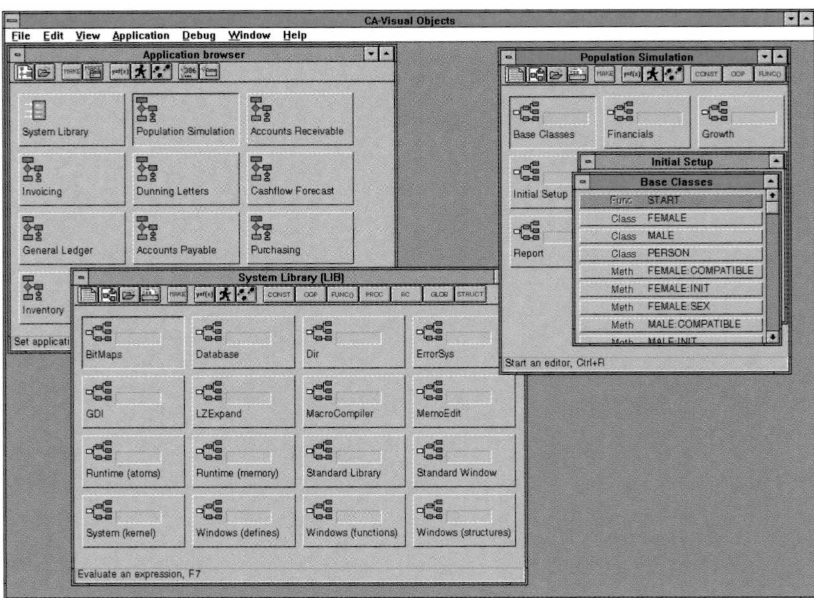

The repository in the CA-Visual Objects development environment is based on a hierarchical object-oriented view of an application. It presents component browsers in an MDI-oriented user interface.

Library Organization

The repository is based on a hierarchical, object-oriented view of an application. Applications (such as "Population Simulation" in the illustration) and libraries (such as "System Library") consist of modules (such as "Base Classes") which consist of entities (such as "Class Female" and "Method Female:Compatible").

Modules are containers of things. A module is somewhat similar to a program file in that it contains a group of presumably related parts of the program. In addition, a module may be used as an encapsulation and scoping boundary, limiting visibility of variables, functions, classes, etc.

Each module consists of *entities* such as:

- constants
- data types
- structures
- variables
- windows
- dialog boxes
- menus
- classes
- procedures
- functions
- methods
- icons
- strings
- reports

The entities are of different types: program entities such as procedures and variables, visual entities such as windows and menus, and resource entities such as icons and text strings. Each entity type has a specific editor and compiler. Custom entity types may be added to the repository. (Chapter 14 describes the standard editors and the extensible architecture.)

The repository holds not only the definition of the entities, but also the information on the dependency relationships which is at the heart of the fast "make" facility. Providing incremental compilation with entity-level granularity, the compiler and repository together provide a highly efficient platform for iterative development.

Application Browsers

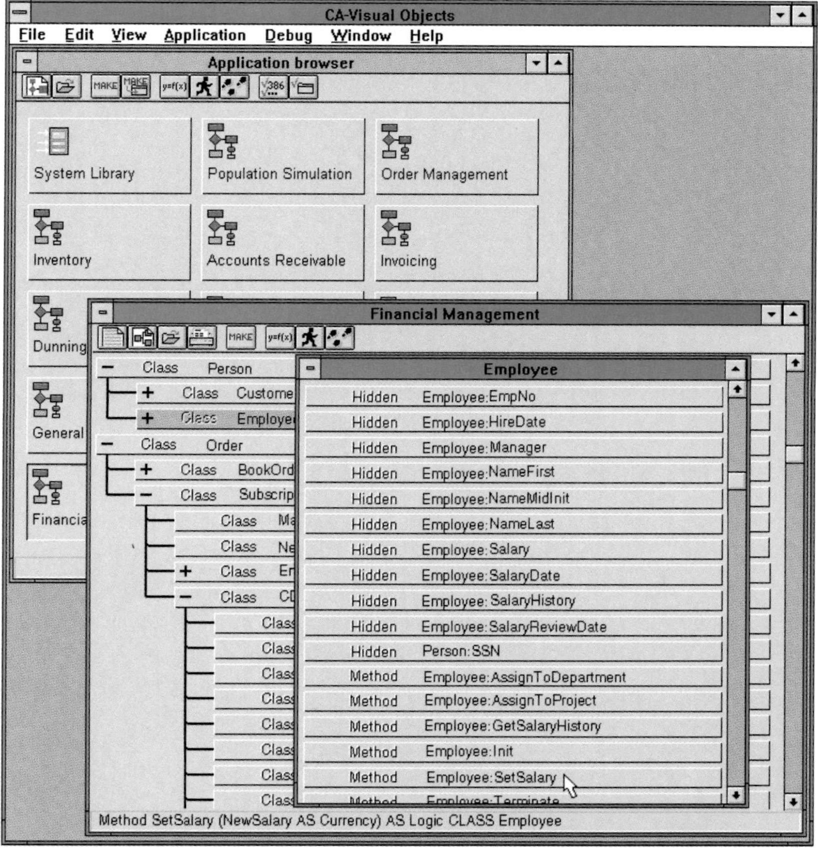

The class browser displays the class inheritance structure in a tree representation, and displays the data attributes and methods of a selected class in a separate "inspector" window. Note the method prototype optionally displayed in the status bar as the mouse moves over an entity in the browser.

Among the most important components of an object-oriented development environment are effective browsers. If code reuse is to be practical, it must be easier to find an application component and all its specifications than to build it from scratch. The application browsers must provide facilities for searching based on names, contents and different kinds of relationships.

The entity browser, the basic framework of the system, presents the components of the application based on "containership": which components are contained within which, from a storage perspective as well as from a scoping perspective. It allows the opening of any component at any level of the hierarchy in a separate window, and lists all the components within each module. Filters permit the restriction of the listing to only interesting components, and searching facilities aid in locating specific entities.

In many cases, a logical structure such as the class hierarchy, the function call structure or the dependency structure may be more useful. The IDE provides logical browsers that display the components of the application in such a logical view.

The most important is the class browser, which displays the class inheritance hierarchy in an easily manipulated tree representation. Subtrees may be expanded or closed in a simple outliner metaphor similar to that used in most file management systems. Any class may be inspected with a detailed listing of its components: the data attributes (hidden and exported instance variables) and the methods. The components can include all inherited components or just those owned by the class itself.

The object-oriented repository supports the "property inspector": click on an object with the second mouse button, and a local object menu lists the things that can be done to that kind of object.

Rearranging the contents of the repository is done through direct manipulation using "drag-and-drop" techniques. For example, to move an entity such as a function to another module, simply drag it over between the two MDI subwindows. Similarly, to copy a module to another application, simply drag the entire module over. (Note that replicating entities or modules is not normally required, as the system supports repository-wide sharing of entities with applications specified in a search path.)

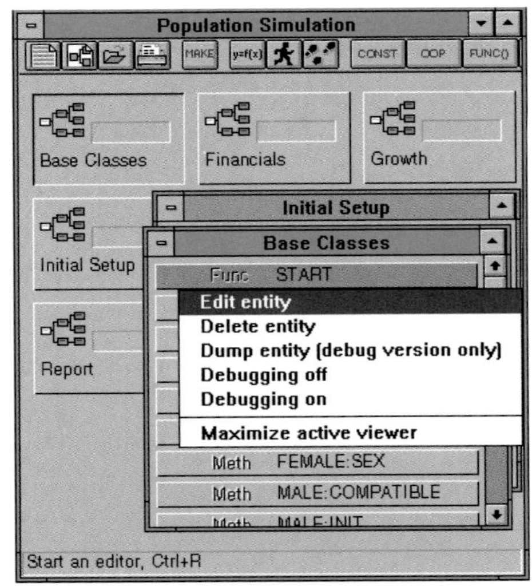

The "property inspector" brings up a local menu of the operations available for each kind of object.

Life Cycle Management

The repository is closely integrated with the development tools, and is configured as a local resource manager for each developer. To enable workgroups to cooperate over a network, the repository is extended to support sharing of components and cooperative development of an application.

Cooperative development requires robust life cycle management tools, such as library management, change management and version control. The CA-Visual Objects repository is integrated with library management technology from CA-PAN/LCM which provides such control across an entire network and even across mixed environments. (See Chapter 7 for a description of the functions of the life cycle tools.)

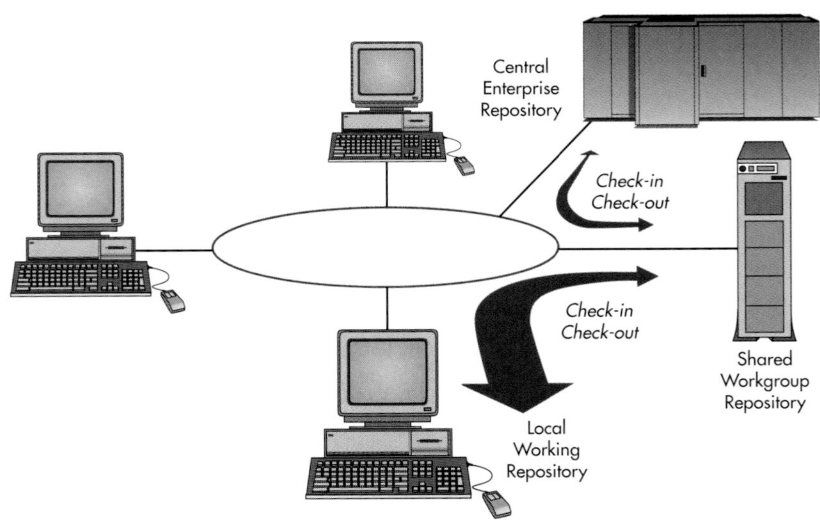

Distributed life cycle management helps a workgroup manage the application components they cooperate on. Each developer checks out components from the network repository, and checks them back in; complete applications may be kept in a centralized enterprise repository on a mainframe, with automatic version and configuration management.

CHAPTER 14

Visual Workbench

The Visual Workbench of the CA-Visual Objects architecture provides an Integrated Development Environment that simplifies the creation of GUI applications and eliminates the need to write code for the visual components. It specifically supports the iterative development paradigm. The IDE forms a productive framework for the development of all kinds of applications, including mission-critical systems.

The development environment provides visual development tools, code generators, editors, compiler, linker, debugger and an integrated, object-oriented repository. It relies on the facilities of the underlying foundation: the object-oriented compiler and support system, the life cycle management tools, and the client/server and database facilities. The architecture is extensible, allowing clients and third-party developers to add new entity types to the system, with editors and compilers fully integrated with the repository and the workplace shell.

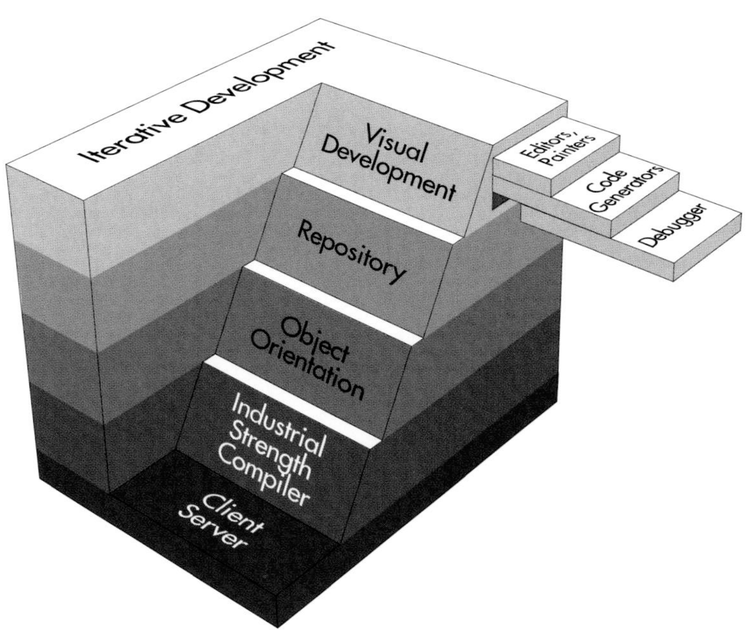

The Visual Workbench includes visual development tools as well as code generators and debuggers. It is closely integrated with the repository.

Visual Development Tools

It is certainly possible to build graphical user interfaces by programming directly, either with procedural code or, preferably, using the object-oriented architecture of CA-Visual Objects or C++ together with the GUI class library CA-CommonView. But visual development tools such as form and menu painters provide a more productive and effective way. These systems allow the definition of both the visual appearance of an application and the actions and data elements that correspond to its "controls" (menu items, buttons, data fields, etc.).

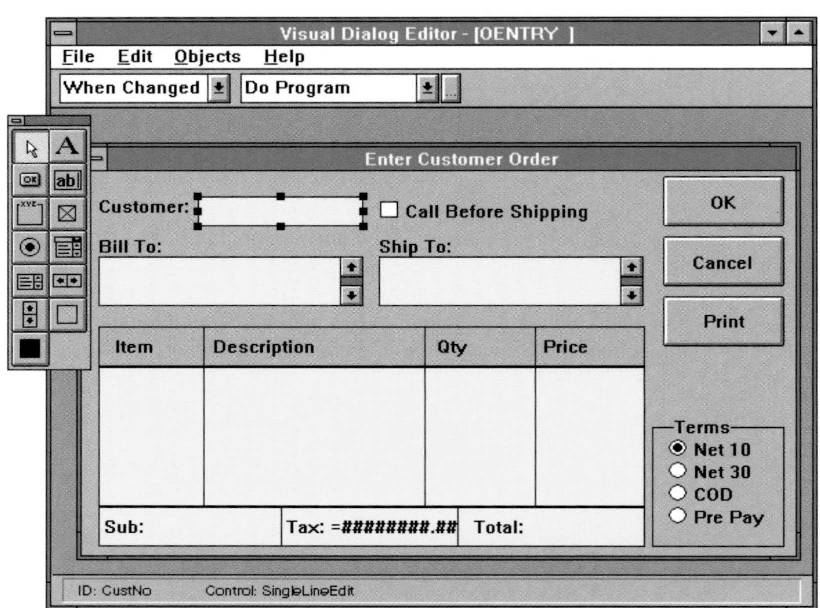

The form painter lets the developer define the visual aspects of the user interface in a WYSIWYG environment. A code generator converts the painted form into well-structured source code.

The visual development paradigm is used not only for laying out the visual appearance of windows, forms and dialog boxes, but for specifying processing code as well. The event-driven paradigm of GUI programming makes it natural to define the entire program, with all its code, in terms of "event handlers" that hang from the controls of the user interface. These are processing modules designed to handle the events that can occur with all the elements of an application.

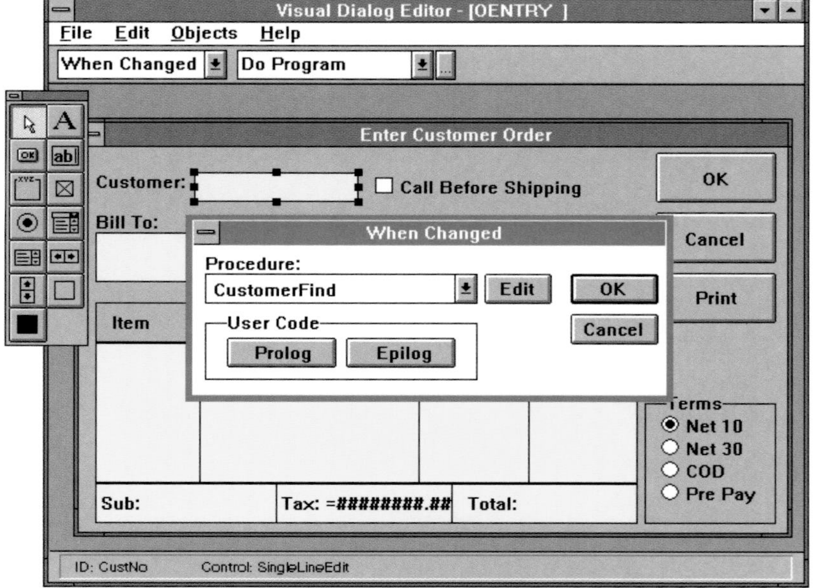

The attributes of a control include code to be executed at various events.

An "event" can be anything that happens, from a mouse click or a keystroke to a database retrieval or a message from some program. Note that GUI programs are supposed to be very responsive, typically responding on a keystroke level. For example, an OK button may be "dimmed" or "grayed," which means the operation is unavailable, as long as some file name field is empty. After the first keystroke into the file name, the OK button becomes available—provided the file name is valid! Indeed, the source code editor of the CA-Visual Objects development environment analyzes the program code for every keystroke, invoking the parser component of the compiler, marking up and color-coding the program according to its structure.

The needs of business applications are different from those of a development system, but keystroke responsiveness remains fundamental to the GUI paradigm. Data entry validation may be done on a keystroke level or, more likely, on completion of entry for the field (the "loss-of-focus" event). Lookup of valid values, in the database or in tables held in the program, may be done with special buttons and key codes or, in some cases, during data entry on a keystroke level. The processing of the transaction, with global data entry validation and database operations, is handled by the "click" event handler for the OK button.

The window and dialog box painter of the CA-Visual Objects IDE (and of other Windows application development systems such as CA-dBFast and CA-REALIZER) provide support for a number of standard events, such as get- and lose-focus, keystrokes and mouse events. They also provide a number of built-in standard actions, such as "forward to next record" or "go to the end of the file." In addition, they provide facilities for execution of custom code, either newly written code or a reference to existing code in the repository. Standard actions and existing functions may be combined with prolog and epilog processing—this extends the flexibility of the system while promoting the reuse of standard operations. The specification of all these event handlers is done entirely with a point-and-click interface. The flexibility of the event handler paradigm is such that quite complex applications may be generated this way. Some of the actual event-handling code must be written by hand, of course, but much of the drudgery of GUI programming is automatically taken care of.

The visual development tools provided in CA-Visual Objects, CA-REALIZER and CA-dBFast operate in a WYSIWYG (What-You-See-Is-What-You-Get) mode, presenting the actual appearance of the application during its development. This approach is invaluable for prototyping, iterative development and Joint Application Development with end users.

The menu editor works the same way: a visual painter allows the definition of the menu structure of the program, and the actions to be taken for each menu item, specified the same way as the actions for window controls. The specifications for the menu include help text and "accelerator" (shortcut) keys such as Ctrl+P for print.

These windows, dialog boxes and menus are stored as separate entities in the repository. When opening a visual entity by double-clicking on it, its corresponding editor is the visual painter rather than the source code editor.

Code Generators

The visual development tools are integrated with a code generator that produces a well-structured GUI program. It exploits the object-oriented architecture of the underlying system and the supporting CA-CommonView class library, generating powerful subclass definitions and straightforward code that uses these classes. The generated code is not only efficient and powerful, it is clean and maintainable and forms a solid foundation for the future evolution of the application.

Under normal circumstances, the generated code can be ignored. The visual development system includes provisions for explicitly specifying the "custom code" that processes all the events that can occur. The code generator simply assembles this custom code into an orderly program structure that handles the minutiae of GUI programming. A visual entity such as a window or menu can be viewed as a black box, albeit a complex one that contains a lot of internal structure and code fragments. The visual entity may be compiled and executed as a whole.

In some circumstances, however, a developer may want to work with the generated code. A special function of the development system allows access to the generated entities, the classes and methods that create the window and its controls. Because the generated code is object-oriented, it is well structured and quite unlike the often horrible output of traditional code generators.

Visual development tools combined with code generators traditionally do not respond well to manual modification of the generated code: the modifications are lost if the window is modified in the visual painter and new code is generated. The object-oriented architecture of CA-Visual Objects has three important features that alleviate this problem. First, the problem is less likely to occur since the event-handler paradigm is flexible enough to handle most real-world situations. Second, modifications may be handled by subclassing the generated classes, cleanly separating the modifications from the generated code. Third, the fine granularity of the automatic "make" facility prevents modifications to one method from invalidating regeneration of the entire class structure. Modifying the code for a specific event-handling routine will cause a conflict warning on regeneration *only* if that particular event handler is affected on the painter level.

Application Generator: CA-TELON

Application generators exploit the fact that most business programs share major structural elements, differing only in the specific processing of the data. They allow the developer to specify, in COBOL, BASIC, Xbase or a nonprocedural, high-level language, the unique code fragments that are required for dealing with unique business needs. These code fragments are then fitted into a standard structure suited to each kind of program, be it GUI-based, conversational, pseudo-conversational, batch or server-oriented. An effective technique for code reuse, generators reduce wasteful "reinventing of the wheel"; they also reduce testing and maintenance costs since the automatically generated standard code is bugfree and only the custom code, usually a small part of the program, needs debugging.

CA-TELON is the leading application generator for commercial mainframe programs. It generates COBOL and PL/I code for several platforms and databases, from mainframe to UNIX to PC systems. The generated applications are character mode, block mode or batch. See Chapter 8 for a description of CA-TELON for legacy systems.

CA-DB:GENERATOR is a nonprocedural application generator for VAX/VMS and UNIX systems. A similar strategy to that described here for CA-TELON will provide migration to the new technologies and environments for CA-DB:GENERATOR clients.

Generation Of GUI Applications

For the new environments, CA-Visual Objects for TELON combines the power of CA-Visual Objects for COBOL with the established strength of CA-TELON to provide a high-level generator of GUI applications. Based on the standard CA-Visual Objects technology, it generates object-oriented, GUI-based, client/server applications from a repository-based, visual development environment.

But unlike the standard code generator built into the visual development tools, which deals with individual entities, the application generator has an understanding of the entire structure of a well-designed GUI-based business application. It allows the specification of the action processing in a high-level, nonprocedural transaction description system, or as procedural COBOL code.

Distributed Application Generation Environment

To provide for generation of the mixed platform, distributed systems that will provide the growth path for many legacy applications, CA-Visual Objects for TELON on the workstation integrates with CA-TELON on the mainframe. The system can generate client/server applications that use a Remote Procedure Call (RPC) implementation to invoke transaction processing code on a remote server system.

CA-Visual Objects for TELON handles the generation of the client side of the application using the standard visual development tools. It is also capable of generating the server component that executes on mainframes, UNIX systems, OS/2, CICS systems or any other of the target platforms of CA-TELON. If preferred, the standard CA-TELON may also be used to generate the server code.

Dictionary and library integration between the workstation and mainframe development systems creates an integrated, distributed development environment that ensures the coordination of the generated application components.

Note that application-level server processing may be a useful paradigm, even when all parts of the application operate on the same system. GUI applications must be responsive and cannot "go away" to do a large amount of business processing. When such processing is required, the best solution may be to spawn a separate process and let the GUI program continue independently, going about its business. See Chapter 15 for a more detailed discussion of distributed processing.

Distributed Development Environment
Client/Server Execution
CA-TELON
Generated Server Application
COBOL
Dictionary Integration
Remote Procedure Call
Generated GUI Client Application
CA-Visual Objects for TELON
CA-Visual Objects for COBOL

The distributed development environment for CA-TELON mirrors the execution environment of the GUI client/server application. CA-Visual Objects for TELON generates the GUI front-end; dictionary integration provides coordination with the server generator.

Editors

All component editors are brought up directly from the browsers: simply double-clicking on an entity opens the corresponding entity editor in a subwindow. The editors include the source code editor, a menu definition system, a form (window) painter, icon and string resource editors, and the CA-RET report painter.

The editor is closely integrated with the object-oriented repository, and does not use a file-based paradigm. Entities

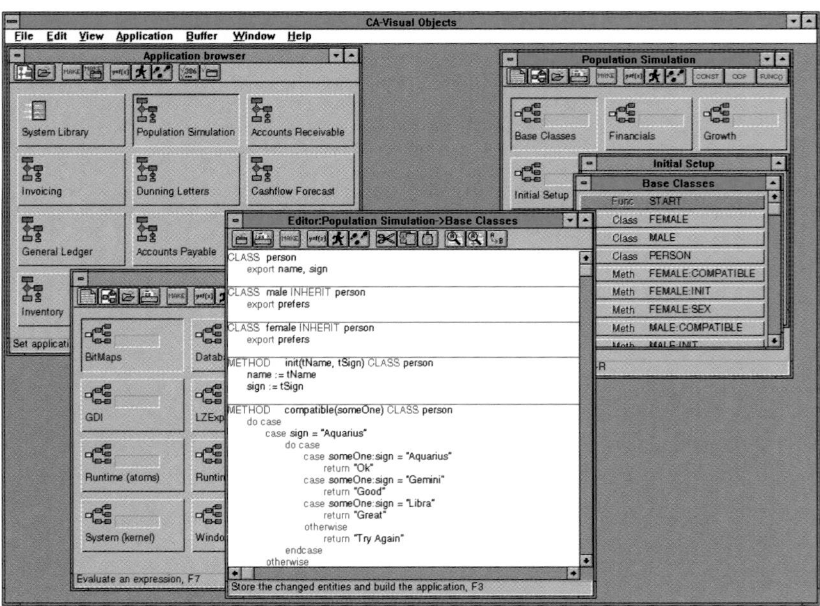

The editors are brought up directly from the IDE browsers. Here, a source code editor has been loaded with a selection of entities from the entity browser.

(procedures, functions, methods, classes, etc.) may be loaded into the editor at any time, in any order. The editor of course also supports the use of external files.

The source code editor draws much of its strength from its close integration with the repository. At any time, it can draw on the information in the repository to display information about a class or function referenced in the source code. The editor can complete a partially entered statement, filling in the parameters defined in the prototype of a function or method. It is also closely integrated with the compiler, and invokes its parser component for every keystroke. Based on this continual parsing, the editor color-codes the source code based on its structure.

Query Editor

The CA-QbyX query system uses the Query By Example model for database operations. It also supports direct SQL entry, or editing of the SQL statement that is automatically generated by the Query By Example facility. CA-QbyX can operate standalone, and supports generation of forms-based applications using its visual form editor, nonprocedural database operations and simple scripting language.

CA-QbyX is also used as a query editor in the CA-Visual Objects systems. It allows generation and test execution of all kinds of database operations, queries as well as update, insert and delete operations. The generated queries may be used in applications.

With relational database processing, the query editor has a particularly important role in support of other components of the system. Complex queries may be defined and tested in the query editor, saved in the database as views, and transparently used as virtual tables in applications and reports. Both the CA-RET reporting system and the custom controls that support database lookup provide built-in facilities for specifying database queries, but for complex queries with nested subqueries and similar features, the systems can draw on the power of CA-QbyX.

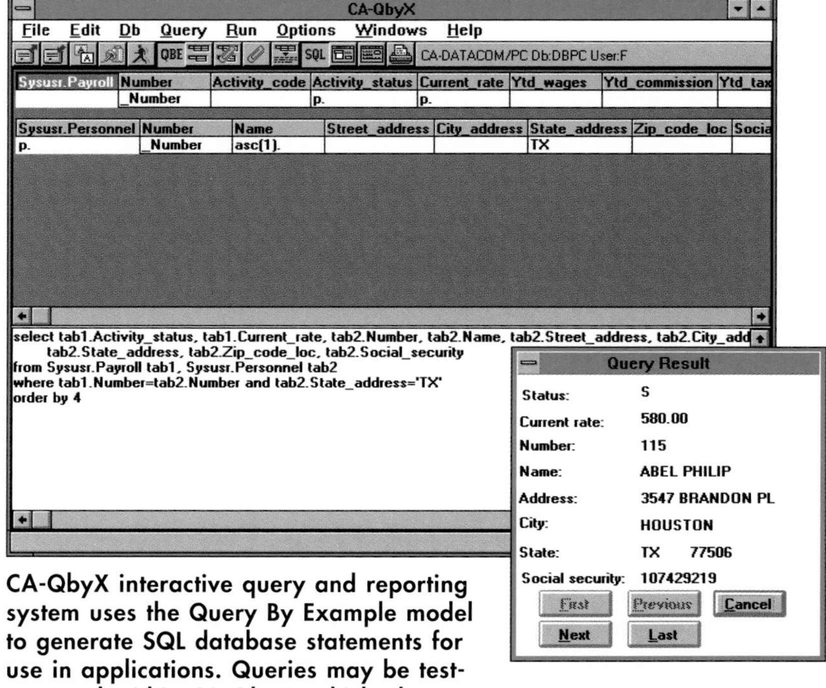

CA-QbyX interactive query and reporting system uses the Query By Example model to generate SQL database statements for use in applications. Queries may be test-executed within CA-QbyX, which also supports standalone operation.

Report Editor

The reporting system of CA-Visual Objects is the powerful CA-RET system, with full support for fonts, graphics and advanced layouts; it is described in more detail in Chapter 16. CA-RET reports may be executed standalone, and may also be invoked from an application—in that case, the report engine can run as a background task while the application goes about its business.

The report editor is the standard WYSIWYG CA-RET report definition system: from the perspective of the CA-Visual Objects repository, a report is an entity like any other, and the editor for the entity is CA-RET. The editor also connects with the code generator to produce the object-oriented code used to invoke the report from the application.

Debugger

The debugger of the CA-Visual Objects architecture provides functions such as single-stepping in the source code, breakpoint handling and editing, and inspection of variables at runtime. Operating in a multiwindow, multitasking environment, the debugger can present source code and data information in one window while allowing the application to execute in another window. Note that the debugger does not require a dual monitor configuration.

The debugger exploits the multitasked environment to allow testing of multiple applications at the same time. This is of crucial importance, since the application will eventually operate in a multitasked environment and its behavior in the real world must be checked. For example, the debugging system allows the checking of two applications that interact by means of DDE: the two applications can operate in separate windows, with the debugging sessions in two other windows.

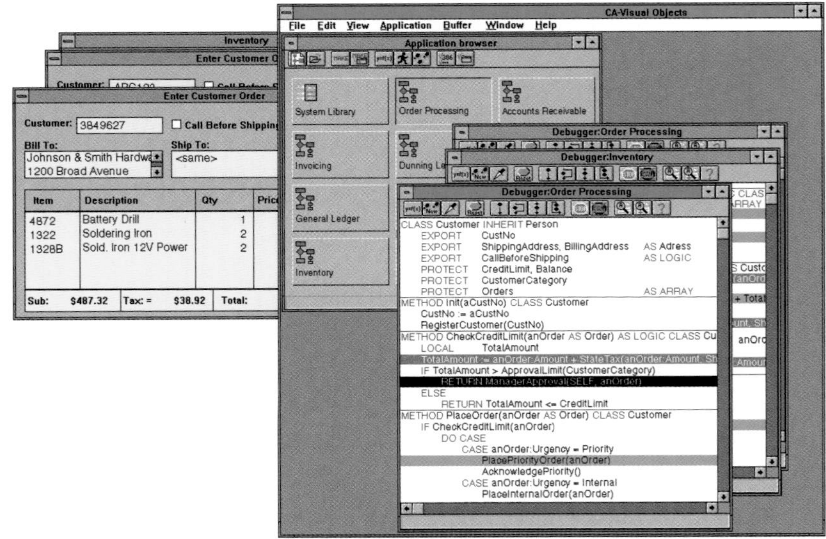

The CA-Visual Objects debugger operates in a subwindow, allowing source code, data display and the executing application to coexist in other windows.

Extensible Architecture

Object orientation provides a convenient and reliable way of extending applications and application libraries, through the use of class libraries. In the same way, the object-oriented repository and visual workbench of CA-Visual Objects are extensible, allowing clients and third-party tool developers to add new entity types and custom subsystems.

When a new entity type is registered with the system, it can have an "editor" and a "compiler." These are high-level conceptual terms: the "editor" is some tool that is used to create or modify the entity, and the "compiler" is some tool that is used to prepare the entity for execution. The editor and compiler for ordinary source code entities are obvious. The flexibility of the architecture is illustrated by the way visual entities are handled and the visual development tools are integrated in the system.

For forms (windows and dialog boxes), the "editor" is the graphical form painter, which allows the specification of the appearance of a form, the object-oriented attributes of the form and its constituent controls, and the event handling operations including custom code. The "compiler" for a form is the code generator, which in turn stores its results in the repository and invokes the standard code compiler to turn it into something executable.

The integration of reports is even more interesting. In this case, the editor is the report painting component of CA-RET, which is a complete subsystem that can also operate standalone. A compiler is not required for the report itself, which is ready to execute once defined; however, the compilation step includes a code generator which produces object-oriented code that invokes a report execution from an application.

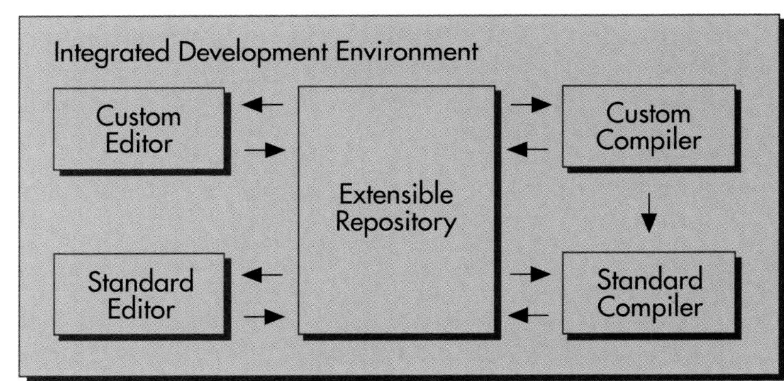

The extensible CA-Visual Objects architecture permits the definition of new entity types in the repository, each with its own custom editor and custom compiler. A custom compiler can include a code generator or preprocessor and can invoke the standard compiler for the final step.

For "resource" entities such as icons and text strings, the editors are specialized tools built into the IDE, and the compiler is a specialized tool that converts the high level resource definition to the native resource file format of each GUI platform.

This architecture provides a very robust framework for extending the development environment. Combined with the extensibility inherent in the object-oriented system, and the direct support for external utilities in the form of DLLs and external programs, it opens the CA-Visual Objects architecture to any kind of development tool and any kind of processing function. It lays the foundation for a vigorous third-party industry that can take the system to unanticipated heights.

CHAPTER 15

Distributed Processing

In the increasingly complex, networked computing environment, and in the increasingly decentralized business world, distributed processing is a common direction of growth. Developers from each of the three main categories—downsized mainframe systems, networked midrange systems and upsized PC systems—naturally progress to a distributed view of application structures.

Surrounding Host Systems With Workstations

IS organizations with large investments in legacy systems often find that the most productive and immediately effective way of exploiting new technologies while protecting investments is to "surround" host applications with workstations. The host system does what it is best at—high transaction rates, large data volumes, heavy batch processing—based on existing code; the workstation contributes its unique advantages in terms of user interfacing and immediate response; and the combination is produced with minimal effort and disruption.

However, in most cases this architecture is no longer implemented through simple "front-ware": thin user interface layers in front of unchanged 3270 applications. Temporarily popular in the early years of GUI workstations, this stop gap approach has now fallen out of favor. Most developers want to place more than user interfacing on the workstation: a modern desktop machine has plenty of processing power and can contribute more than just cosmetics.

Workstations should be able to operate independently, with much of the data validation and calculations expected of the complete systems. Transactions may be committed only when the workstation connects to the host, perhaps online during normal work, perhaps overnight through uploading of job batches.

These types of system architectures may incorporate different kinds of distribution. The workstation may operate online with normal transaction processing; it may execute remote database operations; it may download database selections, process them and upload job batches using simple data transfer and job submission.

In order to construct systems for this kind of "independent workstation" architecture, developers usually need to be able to incorporate legacy code in the workstation. Both developing and maintaining such a system, with identical and synchronized processing on both platforms, is very demanding. It requires the strongest technical facilities for the actual construction of the system, and the most comprehensive life cycle management tools for keeping the entire system under control.

CA-MASTERPIECE with CA-MASTERSTATION is an example of a system with this architecture. The center of processing and the holder of the central database is a host system, which might be a mainframe, an AS/400, a VAX or UNIX system. Windows-based workstations allow data entry and complete processing of functions, such as Accounts Payable, which are validated against downloaded database extracts and posted to the centralized ledger when convenient.

Upsizing PC Systems

A natural way for PC solutions to grow is to incorporate some form of distributed processing over a Local Area Network. Larger, mission-critical applications by definition involve data sharing among several users. As the number of users, the data volume and the transaction rate grow, simple file sharing cannot meet performance and throughput demands. The most straightforward solution is the client/server database, operating on a powerful PC server. This technology can give otherwise standard PC solutions many of the performance, security and integrity characteristics of traditional industrial-strength systems.

To optimize the use of the client/server architecture, thereby maximizing performance and ensuring integrity, more and more processing is transferred to the server. As the server grows into a UNIX/RISC system, an AS/400, a VAX or a mainframe, the overall solution takes on more of the characteristics of a traditional system. Indeed, when looking at a system with GUI-based, desktop workstations and a powerful centralized application server, it may be impossible to determine if it originated as a mainframe surrounded by workstations or a network of PCs that invoked processing on a server. The same considerations apply in either case.

ACCPAC Plus Accounting is an example of a system that grows like this. ACCPAC Plus Accounting is widely used as a DOS-based system operating on standalone PCs or on networks with a file-sharing type database on standard file servers. The next generation of the product, ACCPAC Plus Accounting for Windows, provides GUI workstations that operate with a client/server database, including powerful server machines, PCs or otherwise, that support both database and application processing.

The Asymmetric, Heterogeneous Network

Many distributed application architectures have a simple form of symmetry, such as workstations surrounding a central database server. As business requirements for decentralized operation grow and developers exploit the new technologies more fully, application structures become increasingly complex. Systems of different types may operate independently and cooperate as peers.

These asymmetric, heterogeneous network structures involve not only database access and service requests, but message transfers and transaction posting. The distribution of processing is based on many different kinds of communication, ranging from closely coupled messaging such as networked DDE, to messaging through e-mail, to Electronic Data Interchange (EDI) between completely disparate systems over public networks.

CA-UNICENTER and CA-Warehouse BOSS are examples of systems that support asymmetrical heterogeneous networks. They provide different types of administrative services, ranging from removing a user's access privileges across a mixed network to radio frequency communication between a dispatcher and forklift trucks in a warehouse.

Different Distribution Architectures

When rearchitecting a traditional centralized system to a distributed architecture, the system may be split in different ways. The distribution point may be placed between the main functional modules of user interfacing, business processing and database processing, or within one of these modules. Each kind of distribution architecture has its own strengths and weaknesses and its own type of impact on the development process.

Splitting off database processing into a *database server* is the most common way of using the client/server architecture; it is useful and very easy to implement, but has some operational limitations. Many developers prefer to place integrity checks, change propagation and transaction management on the server with the database, and thus, the dividing line where distribution occurs begins to creep back into the business processing.

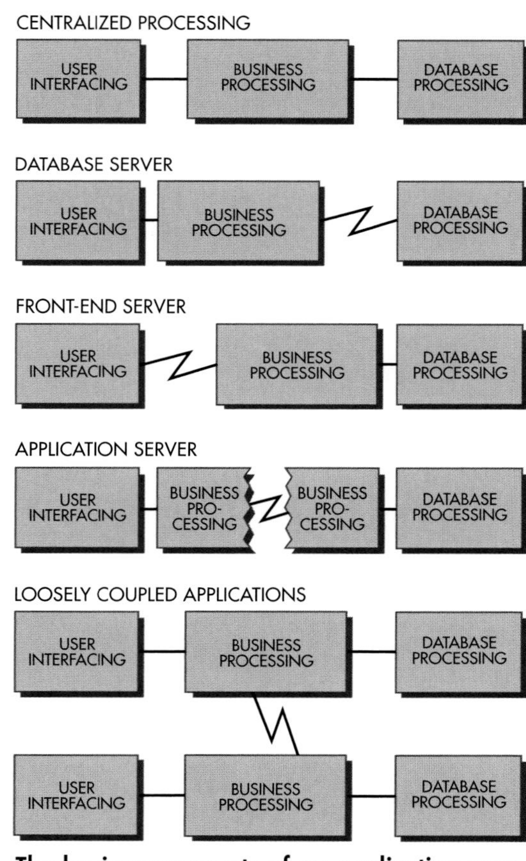

The basic components of an application may be distributed in different ways.

Splitting off user interfacing into a *front-end server* is cost-effective only when the front-end performs some useful processing beyond the pure cosmetics. Again, with more and more processing transferred to the workstation, the distribution point begins to creep into the central business processing component.

Dividing the business processing into two (or more) *application server* parts is the most flexible, powerful and potentially efficient architecture, but also the most demanding to build. Synchronizing processing across several systems, at least anything more complex than incidental services, requires great care in design and implementation—not so much in technical issues as from a business viewpoint.

Finally, *loosely coupled applications,* programs that operate independently but communicate messages or transactions, can tie together various aspects of an enterprise or several independent enterprises. Such a distribution architecture can be very easy or difficult, depending on the nature of the systems being integrated. Since the applications often have different origins, there are often mismatches in data definition that require great care in terms of business design. By comparison, the technical integration issues are relatively simple.

Determining the optimal points to divide an application is a crucial and nontrivial task that is crucial to the overall success of the endeavor. The distribution architecture can have profound implications for the performance, flexibility and maintainability of the system as a whole. Designing the distribution structure requires a thorough understanding of the structure and operating behavior of the application. Implementing it requires powerful technologies that allow flexible packaging of application components and data, and efficient exploitation of basic operating system and network structure. Because it is such a complex and far-reaching decision, designing a distributed environment requires analysis and design tools that go far beyond the purely technical communication considerations. Analysis tools such as CA-COBOLVISION are invaluable in extracting an in-depth understanding of the business processing that is at the heart of the application.

Remote Procedure Call

The client/server architecture is conceptually easy to deal with—indeed, except for the fact that the server is remote, it corresponds exactly to invocation of a service routine within one system, the most basic architectural element in all programming. Thus, many developers prefer this architecture, not only for invoking services from a utility, but also when arranging their own distribution of business logic. The Remote Procedure Call (RPC) is becoming the most widely used technique for application-level distribution.

It should be noted that a system architected around RPC service requests can operate the same way whether the service executes on a separate system or in a separate thread within the same system. This type of arrangement is very useful in GUI environments, where time-consuming processing may be deferred to a separate task where it will not interfere with normal interactive work.

Distributed Transaction Management

Connecting workstations to a mainframe-based enterprise database for transaction processing is different from *ad hoc* query and reporting. The ubiquitous remote SQL access methods are primarily aimed at providing flexibility and convenience in data retrieval, and generally do not provide the transaction management required when running a production application.

Distributed database access designed for production execution must provide complete facilities for transaction management and security. While it is possible to provide such facilities through direct database access, many enterprises are interested in using CICS as a transaction management control center, with CICS OS/2 acting as the gateway between workstations and CICS on a mainframe, an AS/400 or a UNIX system. This architecture is well suited to application-level RPC distribution, since it allows management of both complex database transactions and large business transactions on the remote system. The built-in transaction management facilities of CICS help protect the integrity of the application, and the development systems can take advantage of these facilities.

Development Solutions For Distributed Applications

CA development systems provide integral support for distributed application architectures, using different technologies depending on the design philosophy and intended target of each system.

Client/Server Database

All of the systems support client/server database architectures, through SQL, Xbase DML or the specific access protocols of CA-DATACOM and CA-IDMS. These servers may be accessed through the major public interfaces, such as RDE, DRDA and ODBC, and through static SQL preprocessors when available. See Chapter 4 for an in-depth discussion of client/server database architectures.

One of the key characteristics of a database and development system for distributed architecture is transparency of network configuration. In general, the syntax and semantics of database operations are pretty much independent of database distribution: they exhibit *location transparency*. The database management systems externalize the physical location of data, insulating the application code from address specifics. However, the semantics of database operations are not completely transparent with regard to database location. For example, most relational databases do not allow a join or a subquery to bridge two separate databases on two separate systems, and most do not allow an update transaction to bridge two systems. They do not exhibit *distribution transparency*.

This means that changing the configuration of data distribution often affects application code. Rearranging the distribution of data is the most powerful way to fine-tune the performance of the system as a whole. But as long as such changes in the distribution of data and processing affect application code, network optimization is impeded. The sensitivity of application code to the configuration creates a maintenance burden that can prevent the system administrator from exploiting new technologies and price-performance ratios.

As long as the state of the art of database systems lacks complete distribution transparency, applications must be structured carefully to minimize the maintenance impact of configuration changes. While strict adherence to modular design is as valuable here as in other maintainability issues, the benefits of object orientation are particularly useful in helping the developer insulate the application at large from such database structure dependencies.

Application Level Client/Server

The limitations of "thin" front-ware as a distribution structure are well understood. More than cosmetics should be downloaded to the workstation: certainly data entry validation and lookup tables, but also some calculations and other processing. For example, in an insurance processing workstation, the local system should be able to define all aspects of a policy, calculate the premium and generate a "binder" without online access, even if the corporate database is not available. Thus, the distribution boundary needs to move back into the business processing component.

The limitations of a "thin" database server architecture are gradually becoming recognized as well. Because of the limitations of distribution transparency discussed above, because of efficiency considerations and the possibility of network traffic bottlenecks, and because of maintainability considerations, it is often desirable to move more processing out of the workstation and into the server.

Thus, the natural breakpoint for many applications is somewhere in the business processing component. Indeed, penetrating analysis often shows some natural breakpoints that obviously scream for division. The trick is in identifying them.

Developers need tools that help them recognize the structure of the application and identify these natural breakpoints, which depend on data interdependencies and control flow during execution. The analysis tools of CA-COBOLVISION and the interactive browsers of the CA-Visual Objects IDE are very useful in this analysis.

Automatic Generation Of RPC Structure

While all systems can support Remote Procedure Call architectures, CA-TELON in particular is aimed at this kind of application structure. CA-TELON combined with CA-Visual Objects for TELON provide integrated support for automatic generation of distributed applications based on RPC technology. The application generator allows the specification of the execution location of a subprogram: integral to the GUI application, as a separate thread on the workstation, on a LAN server, or on a remote host. The RPC connection is automatically generated, and the server code automatically uploaded and compiled using the distributed life cycle management system.

Not limited to CA-TELON, the underlying RPC technology enables all CA-Visual Objects systems to invoke application server modules on LAN servers, both PC- and midrange-based. This architecture provides a strong foundation for a major growth path in the new computing environment.

The RPC technology also allows invocation of server functions in separate threads on the same system. This technique is particularly useful for executing large functions that would otherwise have to be reengineered in order not to monopolize the system and break the immediate response paradigm of the GUI environment. As GUI operating systems become more robust in their handling of multi-threading, this approach will facilitate the migration of legacy business logic as service functions in GUI applications.

Messaging

While a number of different techniques are available for messaging between loosely coupled applications, one of the most useful is the DDE protocol. DDE is commonly associated with simple data transfer such as the "Paste Link," used for importing and linking spreadsheets or graphics into word processing documents. This use of DDE has grown into the OLE protocol which internally uses DDE.

However, DDE is capable of much more than this. One of the most useful applications of DDE is to send instructions between applications, even if the data may be transferred through other means. For example, DDE is used to transfer commands between applications written in CA-dBFast or CA-Visual Objects and the CA-RET reporting system. CA-RET normally gets its data directly from the database, but both job instructions and runtime parameters are transferred through DDE.

As DDE is extended to support network links, applications can use DDE to exchange both data and instructions across a network as well as within one system. In addition to the support for the procedural interface to DDE, the class library of CA-Visual Objects provides higher-level facilities for DDE communication.

The Distributed Development Process

The development process must exploit the distributed computing environment, just as the applications themselves do. Successful development tools must actively enable developers to leverage and manage the distributed world. Distributed development provides similar benefits for both legacy applications and new, GUI-based and distributed applications.

Most of the development tools described herein are specifically designed to support a distributed development process. A few deserve special attention.

Distributed Analysis, Debugging And Testing

The program analysis and debugging tools of CA-COBOLVISION operate in a distributed fashion, with the program executing on a target system (which may be a remote host or a separate job in the desktop workstation) and the user interface displayed on a GUI workstation. The workstation communicates with the host system in a very flexible manner, allowing offline analysis and requiring online connection only when downloading analyzed programs or actively debugging on the host.

Distributed Life Cycle Management

The distributed life cycle management system, based on CA-PAN/LCM combined with CA-PANVALET and CA-LIBRARIAN, forms the basis for all the CA development systems. Both the CA-Realia II distributed workbench for COBOL development and the CA-Visual Objects systems for object-oriented GUI development incorporate this technology. It is designed to allow multi-tiered library management, with personal repositories on workstations, workgroup repositories on LAN servers and enterprise repositories on host systems. The life cycle management system automates not only the communication, but also security and integrity control as well as synchronization across the distributed environment.

CHAPTER 16

Man–Machine Interface

As Information Systems technology advances, increasing importance is placed on the interface between man and machine. The external behavior of the technology has become a dominant consideration in terms of ease of use and ease of learning, convenience and flexibility, and quality of display and printing.

Indeed, much of the inexpensive processing power now available is applied to the man–machine interface. Today's powerful desktop workstations spend the majority of their cycles on user interfacing; printers sometimes have more processing power and memory than the computers to which they are attached. End users have stated clearly, by voting with their pocketbooks, that they value ergonomics more than faster processing.

Not only have expectations of user interfaces been raised to new levels, but business solutions are also expected to deal effectively with the unstructured data that previously did not fit in the IS world: handwritten material, drawings, photographs, sound, video, etc. No longer the exclusive domain of "multimedia," this kind of information, increasingly valued for its content, needs to be included in general information processing.

In addition, computing environments have ceaselessly grown in complexity. Not only are multiple operating systems a reality in every enterprise, they are often connected in cooperative solutions. End users expect effective and convenient user interfaces in each environment, compliant with local standards and fully exploiting the specific characteristics of the environment, yet conceptually consistent across the different systems.

These increased expectations and complex environments present a challenge to application developers. New technologies, new techniques and new concepts must be mastered. Traditional programming methodologies do not cope well with the issues of graphical user interfaces and near-typeset quality printing. Business programmers find themselves discussing typefaces, text justification, color models and image quality.

The User Interface and Visualization Services of CA90s provide a foundation for constructing attractive and powerful man–machine interfaces. By relying on an object-oriented architecture and the visual development tools of CA Application Development Software, they allow CA clients to meet the high-end demands in these areas. By providing high-level functions that insulate the developer from the characteristics of each platform, they make multiple platform support feasible and economical.

The User Interface and Visualization Services bring ease of use and development productivity to the entire spectrum of user interfacing tools through advanced technologies for *user interface management*, *graphics* and *reporting* services.

User Interface Management Services

Modern user interfacing techniques, especially the graphical user interface (GUI), have had a remarkable impact on the ease of use and ease of learning of computer systems. The dramatic results are of practical business value: ease of use translates into improved productivity and reduced error rates, while ease of learning translates into lower training costs.

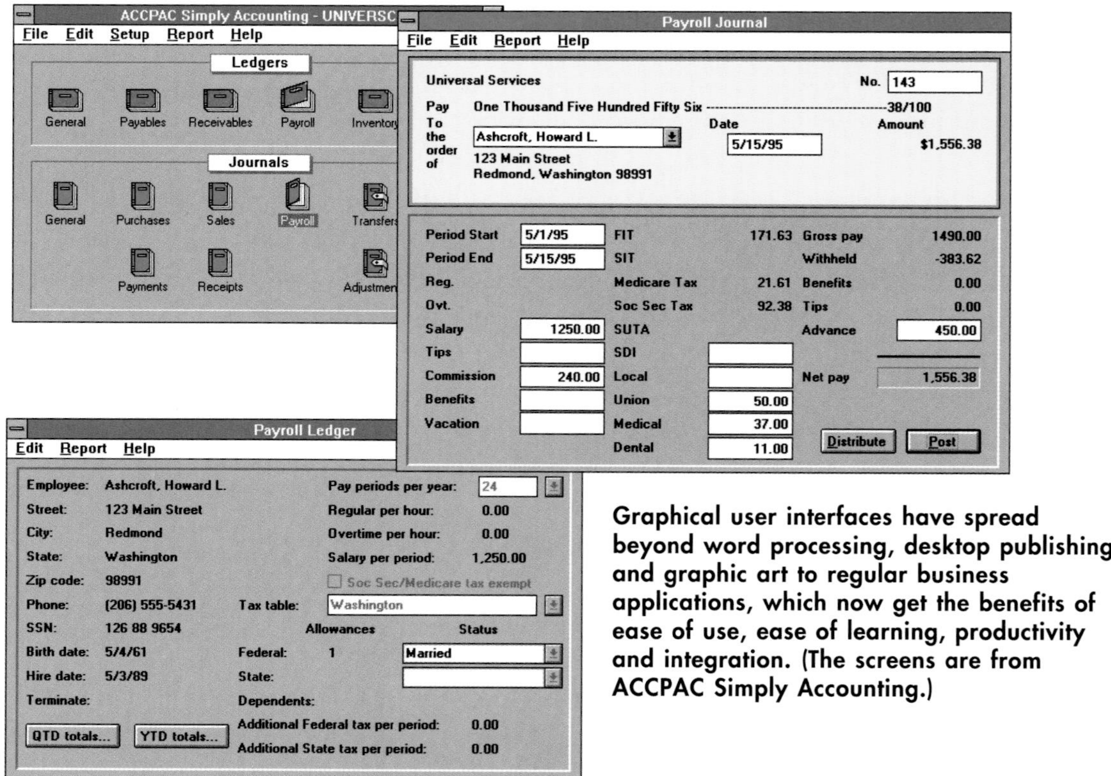

Graphical user interfaces have spread beyond word processing, desktop publishing and graphic art to regular business applications, which now get the benefits of ease of use, ease of learning, productivity and integration. (The screens are from ACCPAC Simply Accounting.)

Originally restricted to the domain of graphics, followed by word processing, desktop publishing and spreadsheets, GUIs are now spreading to mainstream business applications. From data entry in financial applications, to custom query and reporting against business databases, to management tools of all kinds, all the way to the technicians in the "glass house" who run large computer systems and networks, both beginners and experts prefer the ease of entry, convenience and flexibility of the graphical user interface.

But what makes life easy for end users makes life very difficult for application developers. The "illusion of simplicity" presented to end users comes at the expense of much strenuous work. It is commonly estimated that 70 percent of the code in a typical GUI application relates to the user interface. This must be reduced if common business applications are to move successfully to this new world.

And not only is the effort high, the tools and techniques are new. At first glance, GUI programming, with its event-driven structure, appears to pull the rug out from under the feet of developers, obsoleting their hard-won experience.

GUI programming is difficult enough on one platform—portability across platforms is more so. Over the years, the industry has learned how to handle the differences between operating systems, but GUI environments differ more and in more complicated and insidious ways.

Developers need tools that make the move to the new environment manageable. It is the objective of the CA90s User Interface Management Services (CAIUIMS) to address these challenges: to reduce the effort of building modern user interfaces and to provide a common environment for user interface construction across multiple platforms.

The GUI Challenge

Programming for a GUI is a challenge, not only because it is inherently complex, but because the programming paradigm and the tools used are so different from classical procedural programming. The complexity of GUI programs stems from the extremely flexible flow of control, as much as from the graphics functions. In a GUI application, the end user has complete control over the sequence of operations. All operations are interruptible on the spur of the moment and the click of a mouse.

A GUI application should be largely modeless and event-driven. In an event-driven system, the user controls the sequence of processing rather than the program designer. In effect, the program structure is turned inside out—the application is composed of individual tasks that may be executed in any sequence. This flexibility allows end users to work in the nonlinear, often fragmented way that business requires.

This contrasts with traditional methods where the sequence of operations is predetermined. For example, a traditional program, whether operating in block mode (3270) on a mainframe or AS/400, or character mode on a VAX, UNIX or DOS system, displays the screen at specific times, and does not expect to have to do this again during user interaction or calculation. A GUI program must be prepared to repaint the display at any time, not only because of events occurring within this application, but because of outside influences in the multitasking environment. If the user brings up the clock and then removes it, the application must restore the display that was damaged.

Repainting the display "at any time" implies a high degree of timeliness. A well-designed application should respond within a tenth of a second to such events, and should avoid "going away" and putting up the hour glass that implies the application is unavailable. But note that even when the hour glass is necessary, because the application is performing a large task that invalidates all other actions, the program must still yield control with the same level of granularity because the user should be able to get to other applications. Thus, when a program is divided into atomic operations, the size of these operations must be very small. Obviously, dividing up processing in chunks of no more than a tenth of a second is a radical departure from classical paradigms.

Traditional programming techniques can meet these needs, but with high effort. Experienced GUI programmers agree that an object-oriented system combined with visual development tools is the most powerful and most productive environment for GUI programming. Together with CA Application Development Software, CAIUIMS provides such an environment.

Multiple Platform Support

Although appearing similar on the outside, GUI environments are distressingly diverse from a programmer's perspective. Programs that are built directly to the API of the native GUI services require significant rebuilding in order to be ported.

The solution is to design the application to use services with a higher level of abstraction. For example, an application should simply define a menu structure and the action to be taken for each menu selection, and allow the services to manage the different implementations that exist on each platform (mouse, keyboard, accelerators, nested menus, floating menus, tear-off menus, etc.). Such higher level services can deal with all the everyday functions of the GUI without involving the programmer in the specifics of each platform.

By defining the graphical user interface at such a high level, the application can be made *platform-adaptive* rather than just platform-independent. Different systems behave differently and have different standards and style guides. The goal is not to make an application appear identical on each system, but to make it fit the local standards on each platform and simultaneously have a common structure across platforms. At a high level, the application is consistent; at the implementation level, it is appropriate to each system.

Object orientation is a key technology for providing these benefits to application programmers. Services packaged as a "class library" can define behavior in such a fundamental way that it can be common across platforms, while the necessary differences are hidden deep inside the class implementations. CA-CommonView is the standard class library used across all platforms and all languages.

Investment Protection

How can investments in existing applications and expertise be protected in the face of these new challenges, new technologies and new philosophies? How can these investments be leveraged with the new technology?

Implementing new user interfaces with traditional technology often requires drastic changes to the structure of existing applications. Because the GUI paradigm involves much more than cosmetic changes, existing user interface code does not move across very well. However, in most cases it is possible to retain the business logic of the application while restructuring the user interface. The keys to achieving this restructuring in a reasonable and cost-conscious way are object-oriented technology and the analysis tools discussed in Chapter 9.

None of this is feasible unless the new technologies, from object orientation to GUI, are integrated with existing languages and databases. The GUI services are delivered in the form of class libraries which may be used with the object-oriented versions of the dominant languages: C++, Xbase (CA-Visual Objects for Clipper, dBFast, dBASE and FoxPro), COBOL, CA-ADS, CA-IDEAL and CA-TELON.

CAIUIMS Structure

The User Interface Management Services provide a wide range of services, from simple data entry fields and buttons to entire subsystems for validating data entry against a database. The standard user interface services within CAIUIMS are divided into two groups, those that have to do with form (*Presentation Resource Manager* facilities) and those that have to do with function (*User Interaction Manager* facilities). In addition, CAIUIMS provides a number of special functions called *Custom Controls*.

In each GUI environment, such as Windows, Presentation Manager, Motif and others, the underlying system provides a wide range of services. Non-GUI environments are more limited, and often do not even provide a consistent set of device drivers for displays and printers. The *Environment Support Services* provide a uniform foundation for the CAIUIMS services, filling in functions that are missing in specific environments.

While the services provided in CAIUIMS are available using a standard procedural API, the CA-CommonView class library provides the foundation for using object-oriented techniques when developing GUI applications. The visual development tools such as form painters and code generators exploit the object-oriented approach and generate code for the CA-CommonView class library.

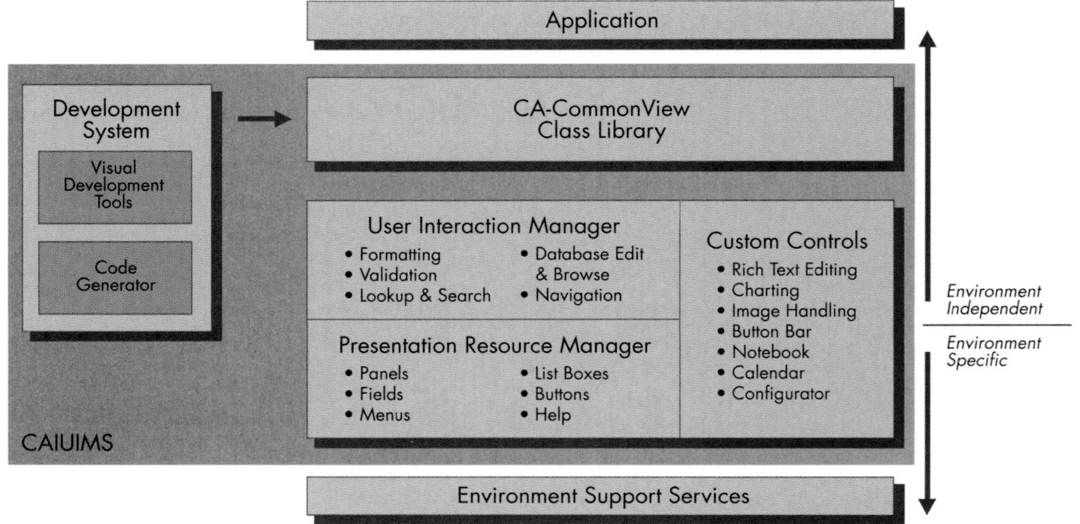

CAIUIMS provides applications with standardized high-level functions across all platforms while exploiting local functions such as those provided by graphical environments like Windows, PM and Motif.

The Presentation Resource Manager

The Presentation Resource Manager is environment-specific: its structure and the extent of its functionality are dependent on the functions and APIs supplied directly by each environment. On GUI platforms, it is a "thin layer" that interfaces to the local API syntax and semantics, since the foundation environment typically provides most of these functions. On any platform where a major function is missing or has non-standard behavior, the Presentation Resource Manager provides the standard features. The functions it provides range from adapting for different screen coordinate systems to a complete help system.

Because GUI systems must be flexible enough to meet the needs of all developers, allowing the construction of graphics and desktop publishing systems, they are of necessity at a rather low level of abstraction, giving the developer full control, but little help. CAIUIMS is aimed at more typical business applications, and the Presentation Resource Manager therefore adds higher level functions than are available in most GUI systems, such as automatic interfacing to help and prompt subsystems.

The User Interaction Manager

The higher level services of the User Interaction Manager are oriented toward application-level functions, such as data formatting, database browsing and searching, validation and navigation. These services, not commonly provided by the foundation GUI environment, often require close integration with applications: for example, to validate data entry, the system often needs to refer to the application database.

The high-level functions provided by the User Interaction Manager include:

- *Data formatting* facilities that provide high-level formatting, including currency formatting for different countries
- *Data validation* facilities ranging from simple data type, range and domain validation to database lookup and exits for custom application-level validation
- *Lookup and search* facilities to help with data entry: it extends the standard pull-down or pop-up menus with sophisticated database search capabilities
- *Database browse and edit* facilities that present a database in convenient spreadsheet format with browse, search, update, insert and delete facilities
- *Navigation* facilities that extend the standard menu systems with keyboard accelerator management, help interfacing and application logic control

Special Tools: "Custom Controls"

The User Interface Management Services are extended beyond their traditional boundaries by a wide range of "custom controls"—facilities that provide some visual presentation combined with some amount of special processing. They can range from a simple utility such as a special kind of button, to a complete service with its own user interface such as a charting subsystem.

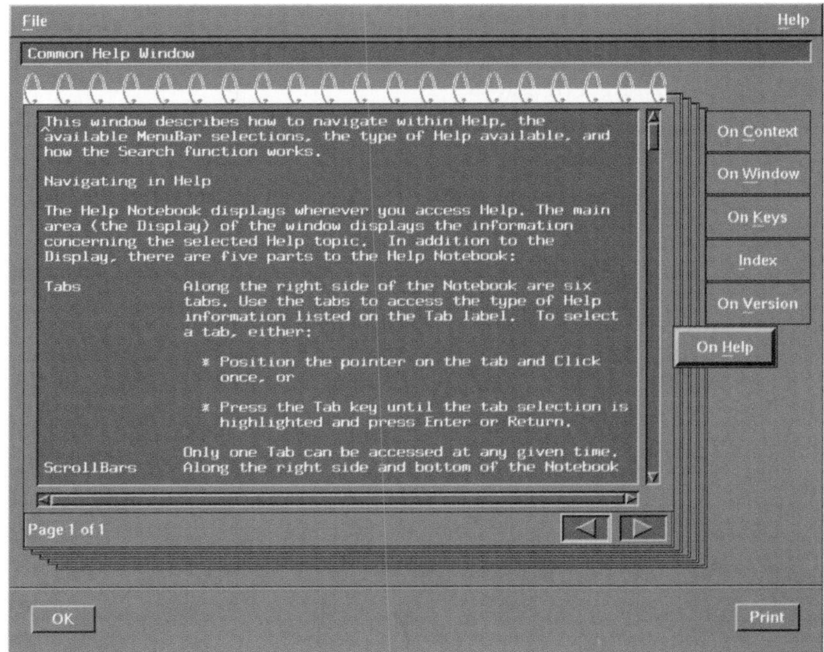

"Notebook" custom control, a part of CUA '91, provides convenient access to a large amount of complex information. Any kind of information may be placed on the pages, as well as data fields, buttons and other controls. In this example from CA-UNICENTER, the notebook is used as a powerful help facility. This is the Motif version; the same facility is provided on other GUI systems such as PM and Windows.

In the more complex cases, custom controls are a convenient way to deliver a large amount of functionality to application developers. Rich text (fully formatted text including fonts, colors, etc.), graphing, spreadsheet and image processing are examples of functions that constitute a major part of some existing product and are repackaged as custom controls.

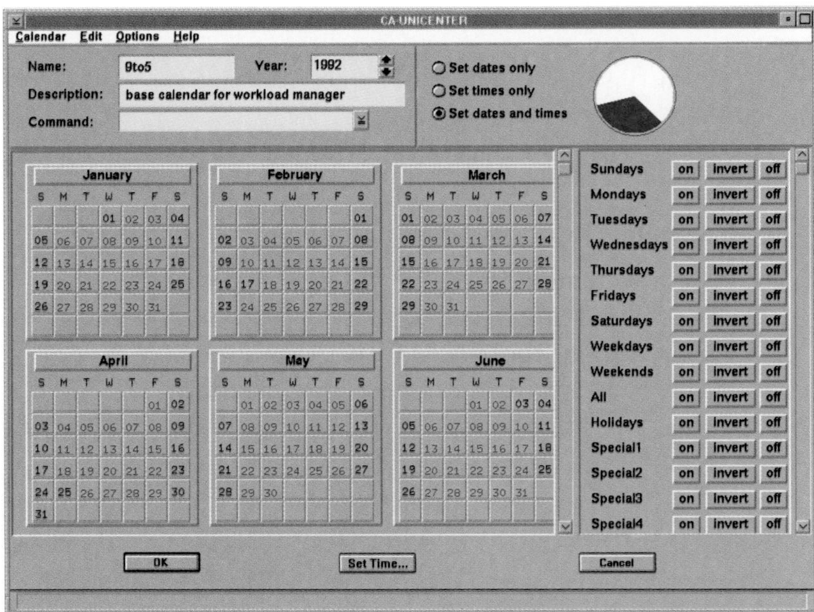

The "Calendar" is a particularly complex and powerful custom control that gives the application access to a complete date subsystem, offering the end user a very comprehensive yet easy-to-use calendar facility. This is the OS/2 PM version.

The custom control concept provides a very simple and well-understood API for any special function. CAIUIMS extends the standard API for custom controls with facilities for letting the custom control register extensive functionality and user interface with the host application. This provides for the intimate handshaking that is required between the two in order to make the custom control appear to be an integral part of the host application. For example, when the end user selects a graph that is overlaid on a form, document or spreadsheet and wants to edit it, the charting subsystem temporarily takes over the user interface providing its own menus, button bars and dialog boxes.

This form of packaging also provides opportunities for performance optimization. End-user customization systems, macro languages and forms-driven systems are often interpretive and exhibit performance problems when asked to handle a complex user interfacing job. By packaging the whole complex subsystem, written in an efficient system programming language, as a custom control, the performance bottleneck is avoided.

Combined with "wrapping" legacy code in a layer of GUI code, this approach can provide the optimal combination of performance, flexibility and development productivity. Some CA products use this technique: ACCPAC Plus Accounting for Windows, for example, combines business logic in COBOL, user interface in CA-REALIZER, and custom controls in C and C++. This hybrid architecture offers the best of both worlds: a user interface built with high-level tools to be easily customizable by clients, combined with the performance and robustness of custom controls and business code built with traditional techniques.

The custom control concept is a cornerstone of the CAIUIMS architecture, and will continue to form the basis for a wide range of extensions to the User Interface Management Services and the applications that use them. The comprehensive services provided in this form give both CA and client applications a common look-and-feel and very strong functionality.

GUI Development Tools

Object-oriented development systems and a GUI class library combined with visual development tools create an optimal environment for GUI development, one that effectively hides the complexities of GUI development.

Class Library

Object orientation is a powerful and efficient application development technique in general, but it is particularly well suited to the requirements of GUI programming. Since a graphical user interface is asynchronous, modeless and event-driven, it is natural to structure a program as independent objects.

The CA-CommonView class library is the delivery vehicle for making the CAIUIMS architecture available to CA client application developers.

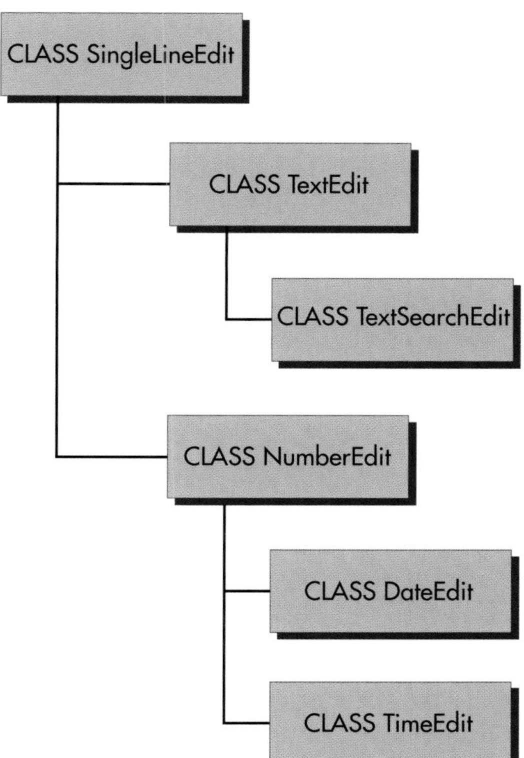

The class library provides hierarchical inheritance trees of increasingly specialized tools that add the higher level functions of the "User Interaction Manager" layer. The structure is illustrated here by the "SingleLineEdit," the GUI equivalent of an ordinary input field. The "TextEdit" provides specialized help, formatting and validation facilities, and the "TextSearchEdit" adds database lookup. Similarly, the "NumberEdit," "DateEdit" and "TimeEdit" provide specialized formatting and validation facilities for those kinds of data. The programmer can draw on precisely those functions required in each case, or add new ones by subclassing further.

The complex structure of a GUI program is hidden away in the class library, allowing the developer to concentrate on the business functions of the program. Complex implementation details such as the "event loop" and the message passing technology specific to each environment is encapsulated by a system programmer into robust, reusable and safely customizable modules, the GUI foundation classes.

The CA-CommonView class library makes applications portable across GUI platforms such as Windows, Windows NT, Presentation Manager and Motif. It also gives them the appropriate platform-adaptive behavior to make the application appear native on each platform and nonetheless exploit the features and capabilities of each environment.

Visual Development Tools And Code Generators

The CA Application Development Software solutions provide visual development tools that integrate closely with CAIUIMS to create a strong development environment for GUI applications. These tools leverage the object-oriented architecture to combine simple development with the flexibility to customize the user interface. In addition to appearance, through simple painting of forms, dialog boxes and windows, the visual development system allows the specification of actions to be taken: standard operations or custom code that extends or overrides the default action of control objects.

An integrated code generator produces the final application, embedding the specified custom code within a standard program structure. Depending on the characteristics of the foundation system, the generated code is procedural or object-oriented. Object orientation is of course the preferred method, since the generated code is more flexible and more maintainable.

Graphics Services

There is little disagreement today about the power that graphical representation brings to information. Endless examples show that an effective interpretation of the information contained in reams of paper can be obtained from a few simple graphs that highlight the fundamental trends and patterns.

Over two decades, the range of graphics handled by computer systems has grown from charts of numeric information, to maps showing geographical patterns, to diagrams showing structural relationships, to drawings illustrating concepts, to images showing real or imagined objects. Today, image processing ranges from simple "fax quality" to full color "photographic quality."

In order to facilitate the use of powerful graphics in CA Enterprise Software Solutions, CA90s defines and incorporates standard graphics services in the User Interface and Visualization Services layer. The graphics technology is available in the form of standalone solutions across a wide range of platforms, from PCs to VAX, UNIX and mainframe systems, and as services integrated with the user interfacing tools of CAIUIMS.

Unstructured Information

By incorporating pictures, computer graphics systems extend the reach of IS to incorporate much of the "unstructured information" that previously did not fit. For many enterprises, essential information was never incorporated in the automated information processing because there was no way to capture, store, retrieve and display it.

The expectations of support for new kinds of information is one of the key challenges of the new environments. Developers must deal with "rich text" (text with full formatting), images (both fax quality and photographic quality), sound, handwriting and video. Originally considered of interest only to "multimedia" applications, education, entertainment and presentations, this new technology is now employed to let ordinary business applications handle all of the unstructured data that does not fit well with classical information technology.

Much work can be expedited, facilitated or made more reliable by including a picture of a person, a handwritten note, a drawing of a part or a photograph of a building:

- Handwritten notes such as insurance damage reports done on the spot, customer complaints, order forms
- Diagrams, drawings, illustrations of products and components
- Photographs of people, locations, situations, products, components
- Spoken notations
- Forms filled in with a pen

The practical benefits are enormous. By handling handwritten notes, we cannot only reduce costs but also give our customers better service. For example, after a customer has sent in a handwritten note with a complaint, a request for service or a warranty claim, we can store the original document for future reference when dealing with the issue.

In addition to image processing, this trend toward dealing with unstructured information incorporates "pen" computing for handwritten notes, sound for voice annotation and messaging, and video animation. The integration of these technologies with general information systems promises even greater benefits as the scope and power of IS expands to accommodate the real needs of the enterprise. Graphics is the most complete and the closest to achieving tight integration with general business systems, but other types of unstructured data are progressing quickly.

Image Processing

Image processing is a very broad term that incorporates functions with widely differing benefits and technologies.

Fax Quality Document Storage

The most basic kind of image processing is document storage, which typically uses fax quality: black and white and relatively low resolution. The benefits lie in automated access to large volumes of information that may not fit in standard information processing. It is clearly very useful to be able to automatically bring up an original check or credit card slip, or the handwritten original insurance claim report, or a diagram of a component or picture of a product being ordered, as an integral part of standard information processing. It can improve service, help end users deal with data and reduce error rates. For example, if the Navy needs part # VS3894786 (a $5 radio tube), it is not good if part # VS3984786 (a transmitter the size of a room) is ordered and sent to a ship halfway around the world, as actually happened during World War II. Today, showing a picture of the part during the order entry process can prevent the mistake.

This kind of image processing presents few technical challenges with regard to the image handling itself. The technologies of scanning, storage, display and printing are well understood. The interesting challenges have to do with integration with business applications, files and databases: if "unstructured information" is to be truly integrated with standard information processing, it must be convenient to store, display and print. Integration of these services with other CA90s services such as User Interface and Visualization Services and Database Management Services will provide the foundation for bringing document processing into standard business applications.

Photographic Quality Image Processing

Photographic quality image processing is a quite different problem. These images are either full range grayscale or color with a high degree of fidelity. They represent faithfully a real object in the real world, or at least a conceived object (the image may be artificial). They are used to present something as it really looks or might look: a person, a house or car for sale, a proposed package design, or the layout of a factory.

This area includes a broad range of technologies designed to address several technical challenges:

- Scanner interfacing for capture of images, in black and white, grayscale or color
- Interface to CD-ROM and video hardware for retrieval and storage of images
- File format translation
- Processing to improve image quality or eliminate extraneous material: sharpening, noise removal, and contrast, brightness and color adjustment
- Editing, retouching, composition or painting of images: image modification can be undetectable
- Compression to reduce the enormous storage requirements (25X compression is feasible)
- Memory and database management for image data
- Effective display of images given hardware limitations
- Effective printing given hardware limitations

Products such as CA-Cricket Image and CA-Cricket Paint provide powerful technology for creating, manipulating, storing, displaying and printing images. In this artificial picture of an art gallery, the floor, the wall and the artwork are all computer generated, except for the two paintings courtesy of Leonardo da Vinci and Alesandro Botticelli which were inserted by computer. The image processing technology is integrated with CAIUIMS in the form of "custom controls."

The built-in functions of common GUI environments do not address these challenges. Standard user interfacing services are certainly capable of displaying a bitmap, but realistic rendering of a photograph on a typical display requires a great deal of sophisticated processing to overcome the limitations of the hardware.

Recent developments in image processing, retouching and painting technology have dramatically advanced the state of the art. Unlike the simple "pixel editors" of the past, these second-generation systems relax technical constraints and allow translucency, air brushing, soft edges and lines thinner than one pixel. In general, they behave like real-world artist tools rather than computer technology.

These image processing technologies, originally developed for products such as CA-Cricket Image and CA-Cricket Paint, are a part of the Graphics Services; they are also packaged as "custom controls" under CAIUIMS. Corresponding facilities in Database Management Services and Application Development Software complete the framework for incorporating photographic-quality images in applications.

Charting

The charting components of CA90s are based on the proven, full-function CA graphics software products that have long been recognized as leaders in the industry for generating high-quality visuals. Producing two-dimensional charts, three-dimensional displays, maps and tables, these services provide the capabilities to present any information clearly and effectively.

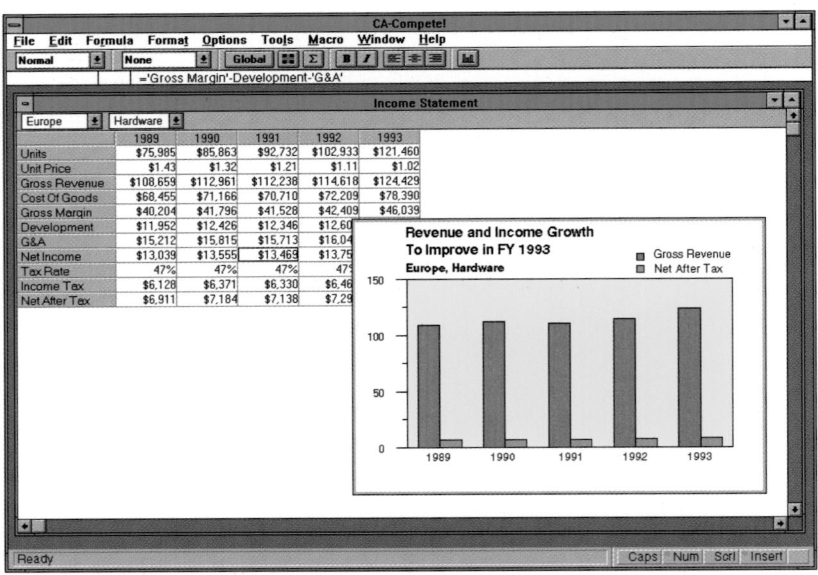

Graph services are packaged as a "custom control," which may be used by any application to present information in chart form on a video display or printer. Here the CA-Compete! multi-dimensional spreadsheet uses an overlaid chart.

Charting solutions for the desktop computing environments include the CA-Cricket products for Macintosh and Windows platforms. Like the imaging services, the charting services are also packaged as CAIUIMS "custom controls" that are utilized in spreadsheets, database and reporting systems, and business applications.

Industry Standards

The Graphics Services not only provide common capabilities across all platforms, they also enable CA solutions to comply with industry graphics standards, significantly extending the functionality of these standards.

CA graphics solutions deliver this portability by utilizing graphics file format translators. This functionality adheres to industry standards to ensure that CA clients can move graphics output from platform to platform without loss of content. Some of the object-based metafile standards supported include CGM (ISO/ANSI), DISSPOP (CA), WMF (Windows), PICT and PICT2 (Macintosh), HPGL (H–P), DDIF (Digital) and GDF (IBM). For image-type graphics, CA software supports and translates between Windows BMP, OS/2 BMP, TIFF, PCX, TGA, PIX, WIN, BPX, GIF, CVP and the new industry standard compression technique, JPEG.

CA graphics utilities also eliminate the incompatibility between graphics metafile types. Through the ability to translate a number of de facto and ANSI standard graphics metafiles, communication is now possible between such diverse hardware/software solutions as graphic arts, Computer-Aided Design (CAD) and business charting.

Reporting Services

Even the most sophisticated online interactive applications will not alleviate the need for printed hardcopy. Some industry observers suggest that the trend is toward a "paperless society" which will be realized through technologies such as Electronic Funds Transfer (EFT) and Electronic Document Interchange (EDI). It is more realistic to expect that these technologies will coexist with the continued requirement for effective and efficient reporting services.

Paper hardcopy in various forms provides the information required to run an enterprise, ranging from detailed operational printouts to executive summary reports. In external relationships with customers and suppliers, paper documentation remains dominant: orders, invoices, acknowledgments, statements, catalogs, reference listings, instructions, etc. Enterprises rely heavily on reports and on their computers' ability to produce them quickly and easily, bringing together all the required information. But changes in computing environments have placed new, challenging requirements on reporting capabilities, such as multiple platform support, modern user interfacing, flexible and comprehensive data access and advanced function printer support.

User expectations of the appearance of computer printout are much higher today than a few years ago. We are no longer satisfied with getting ugly line printer output from line-of-business applications on multimillion dollar corporate systems when a personal system for a few thousand dollars can produce beautiful desktop publishing. Today, even utility bills are enhanced with graphics.

The technology exists to produce high quality reports. The dilemma lies in incorporating this technology within a line-of-business production environment without compromising integrity and security and, equally important, without overwhelming either end users or support staff with the task. Composing a report is much more difficult when you have to deal with different fonts in different sizes, proportional spacing, lines, graphics and all the other new complications. Business people and programmers find themselves getting involved in the typesetting trade, at great cost and inconvenience.

Organizations increasingly consider information a major corporate asset, one that should be used for proactive business purposes to strengthen the enterprise's competitive situation, improve customer service, and make the organization light on its feet so it can respond effectively in a tough economic climate. This means that reporting must be quick. It is no longer acceptable to place a request for custom programming and end up in a multiple month backlog. End users have become accustomed to immediate response from spreadsheet analysis on personal systems, and expect the same response when they utilize corporate data.

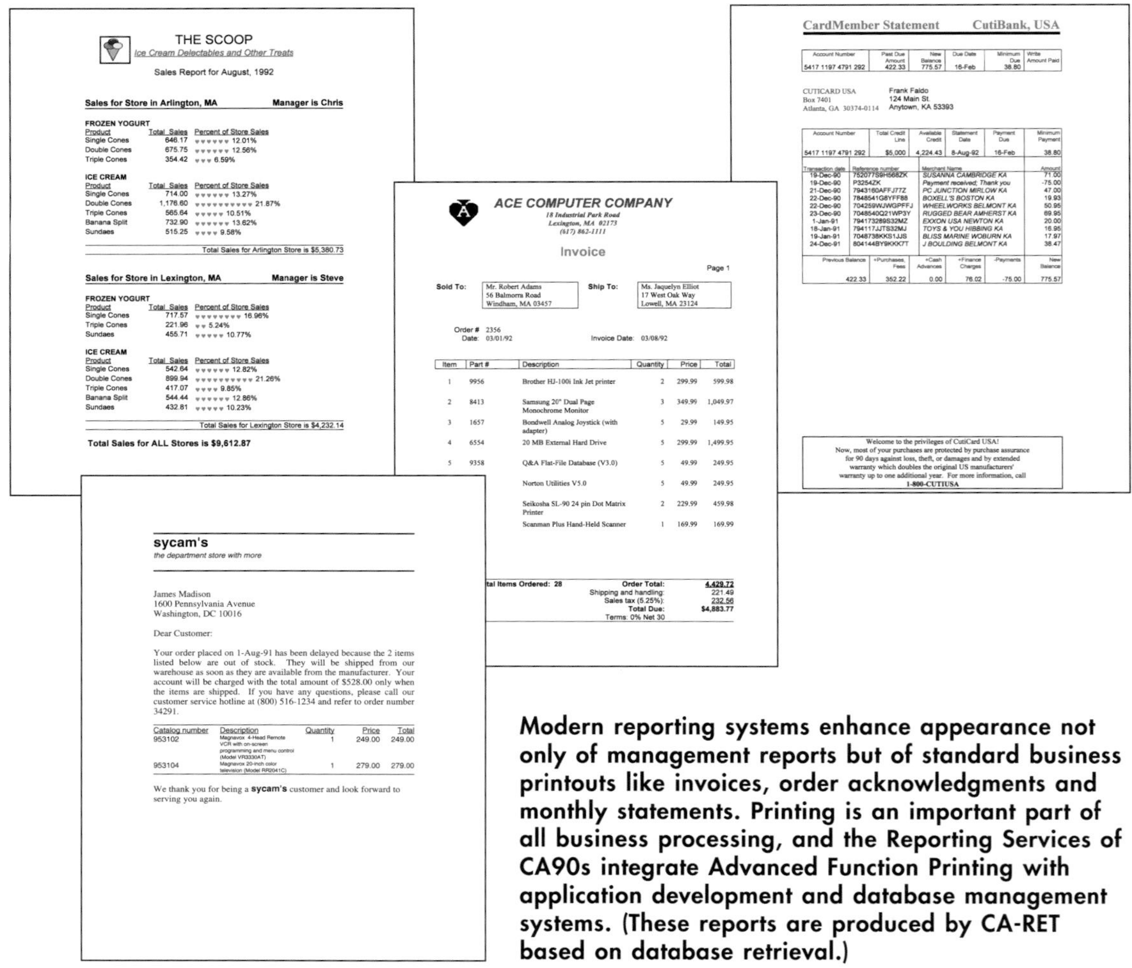

THE SCOOP

Ice Cream Delectables and Other Treats

Sales Report for August, 1992

Sales for Store in Arlington, MA **Manager is Chris**

FROZEN YOGURT

Product	Total Sales	Percent of Store Sales
Single Cones	646.17	12.01%
Double Cones	675.75	12.56%
Triple Cones	354.42	6.59%

ICE CREAM

Product	Total Sales	Percent of Store Sales
Single Cones	714.00	13.27%
Double Cones	1,176.60	21.87%
Triple Cones	565.64	10.51%
Banana Split	732.90	13.62%
Sundaes	515.25	9.58%

Total Sales for Arlington Store is $5,380.73

Sales for Store in Lexington, MA **Manager is Steve**

FROZEN YOGURT

Product	Total Sales	Percent of Store Sales
Single Cones	717.57	16.96%
Triple Cones	221.96	5.24%
Sundaes	455.71	10.77%

ICE CREAM

Product	Total Sales	Percent of Store Sales
Single Cones	542.64	12.82%
Double Cones	899.94	21.26%
Triple Cones	417.07	9.85%
Banana Split	544.44	12.86%
Sundaes	432.81	10.23%

Total Sales for Lexington Store is $4,232.14

Total Sales for ALL Stores is $9,612.87

ACE COMPUTER COMPANY

18 Industrial Park Road
Lexington, MA 02173
(617) 862-1111

Invoice

Page 1

Sold To: Mr. Robert Adams, 56 Balmorra Road, Windham, MA 03457

Ship To: Ms. Jaquelyn Elliot, 17 West Oak Way, Lowell, MA 23124

Order # 2356
Date: 03/01/92

Invoice Date: 03/08/92

Item	Part #	Description	Quantity	Price	Total
1	9956	Brother HJ-100i Ink Jet printer	2	299.99	599.98
2	8413	Samsung 20" Dual Page Monochrome Monitor	3	349.99	1,049.97
3	1657	Bondwell Analog Joystick (with adapter)	5	29.99	149.95
4	6554	20 MB External Hard Drive	5	299.99	1,499.95
5	9358	Q&A Flat-File Database (V3.0)	5	49.99	249.95
		Norton Utilities V5.0	5	49.99	249.95
		Seikosha SL-90 24 pin Dot Matrix Printer	2	229.99	459.98
		Scanman Plus Hand-Held Scanner	1	169.99	169.99

tal Items Ordered: 28

Order Total: 4,429.72
Shipping and handling: 221.49
Sales tax (5.25%): 232.56
Total Due: **$4,883.77**
Terms: 0% Net 30

CardMember Statement **CutiBank, USA**

Account Number	Past Due Amount	New Balance	Due Date	Minimum Due	Write Amount Paid
5417 1197 4791 292	422.33	775.57	16-Feb	38.80	

CUTICARD USA
Box 7401
Atlanta, GA 30374-0114

Frank Faldo
124 Main St.
Anytown, KA 53393

Account Number	Total Credit Line	Available Credit	Statement Date	Payment Due	Minimum Payment
5417 1197 4791 292	$5,000	4,224.43	8-Aug-92	16-Feb	38.80

Transaction date	Reference number	Merchant Name	Amount
19-Dec-90	752077S9H568ZK	*SUSANNA CAMBRIDGE KA*	71.00
19-Dec-90	P3254ZK	*Payment received; Thank you*	-75.00
21-Dec-90	7943160AFFJ77Z	*PC JUNCTION MIRLOW KA*	47.00
22-Dec-90	7848541G8YFF88	*BOXELL'S BOSTON KA*	19.93
22-Dec-90	704259WJWGPFFJ	*WHEELWORKS BELMONT KA*	50.95
23-Dec-90	7048540Q21WP3Y	*RUGGED BEAR AMHERST KA*	69.95
1-Jan-91	794173289S32MZ	*EXXON USA NEWTON KA*	20.00
18-Jan-91	794117JJTS32MJ	*TOYS & YOU HIBBING KA*	16.95
19-Jan-91	7048738KKS1JJS	*BLISS MARINE WOBURN KA*	17.97
24-Dec-91	804144BY9KKK7T	*J BOULDING BELMONT KA*	38.47

Previous Balance	+Purchases, Fees	+Cash Advances	+Finance Charges	-Payments	New Balance
422.33	352.22	0.00	76.02	-75.00	775.57

Welcome to the privileges of CutiCard USA!
Now, most of your purchases are protected by purchase assurance for 90 days against loss, theft, or damages and by extended warranty which doubles the original US manufacturers' warranty up to one additional year. For more information, call
1-800-CUTIUSA

sycam's

the department store with more

James Madison
1600 Pennsylvania Avenue
Washington, DC 10016

Dear Customer:

Your order placed on 1-Aug-91 has been delayed because the 2 items listed below are out of stock. They will be shipped from our warehouse as soon as they are available from the manufacturer. Your account will be charged with the total amount of $528.00 only when the items are shipped. If you have any questions, please call our customer service hotline at (800) 516-1234 and refer to order number 34291.

Catalog number	Description	Quantity	Price	Total
953102	Magnavox 4-Head Remote VCR with on-screen programming and menu control (Model VR3330AT)	1	249.00	249.00
953104	Magnavox 20-inch color television (Model RR2041C)	1	279.00	279.00

We thank you for being a **sycam's** customer and look forward to serving you again.

Modern reporting systems enhance appearance not only of management reports but of standard business printouts like invoices, order acknowledgments and monthly statements. Printing is an important part of all business processing, and the Reporting Services of CA90s integrate Advanced Function Printing with application development and database management systems. (These reports are produced by CA-RET based on database retrieval.)

Access to the relevant data is the cornerstone of reporting. High-level, visual tools are needed that provide the flexibility and power of relational database access, even for data that is maintained by non-relational database systems or indexed file systems.

These sophisticated demands on reporting apply not only to executive level summary reporting, but across the broad range of what "reporting" includes in business computing. A "report generator" is commonly used as a tool to do all printing for business applications, including the printing of invoices, monthly statements, inventory sheets, dispatch schedules and purchase orders. Therefore, we need to combine the flexible and elegant formatting of *ad hoc*, end-user tools with the programmable power and system integration of production reporting systems.

Advanced Function Printing

Printer technology has advanced dramatically in the last decade, providing near-typeset image quality at prices and speeds that are comparable to or better than traditional printers. Laser printers and others capable of providing this high image quality, as well as multiple typefaces, line drawings, graphics and image representation, are referred to as *advanced function printers*.

Information formatted professionally with proportionately spaced characters is not only easier to read and more appealing to look at, it also uses significantly less space. This offers several significant benefits, depending on your perspective: use less paper to print the same information (save money and trees), bring more information into the same space for easier analysis, or leave more white space to produce a more pleasing document.

Traditional report generators provide no support for advanced function printers. Two demanding architectural advances are required to make a report generator support advanced function printers: intelligent device drivers and a change in processing logic.

With proportionately spaced fonts of different sizes, the reporting system can no longer consider the report layout as a character grid. Numbers cannot be made to line up in columns by inserting a fixed number of spaces. Every report element must be

```
REGION    OFFICE                          SALES  %  QUOTA
------    -------------      ----------------  --------

WEST      SEATTLE                          $687       87%
          LOS ANGELES                    $9,234       63%
                             ----------------  --------
          TOTAL                          $9,921       64%

EAST      WASHINGTON DC                 $12,803       93%
          ATLANTA                        $9,113       80%
          BOSTON                        $22,840       73%
                             ----------------  --------
          TOTAL                         $44,756       79%
```

REGION	OFFICE	SALES	% QUOTA
WEST	SEATTLE LOS ANGELES	$687 $9,234	87% 63%
	TOTAL	**$9,921**	**64%**
EAST	WASHINGTON DC ATLANTA BOSTON	$12,803 $9,113 $22,840	93% 80% 73%
	TOTAL	**$44,756**	**79%**

Simple line-printer output is no longer acceptable—modern laser printers have educated us on the value of sophisticated fonts, lines, shadings and graphics. The reporting systems of today need extensive enhancement to support this technology.

designed and placed in terms of its size and position—and the size of a column heading, for example, is not easy to determine, since it depends on the typeface and on which specific printer is used. The report layout system and the execution engine must therefore communicate directly with the device driver and its database of typeface characteristics, inquiring the length of every text string given its typeface characteristics.

This is one reason why a separate reporting system is of even greater value today than in the past. Proportionately spaced fonts completely invalidate the logic of most traditional reporting programs. An application programmer can no longer lay out a report with simple formatting statements in COBOL or Xbase. Short of educating programmers in the terminology and technology of the typographic trade, the only reasonable solution is to rely on a typographically powerful reporting engine.

The CA90s Solution

The solution lies in combining the strongest technologies available: personal workstations and high-level design tools for high productivity and quick turnaround time, graphical user interfaces for taming the complexity of typographical design, distributed laser printers for immediate access, and relational access to production databases to tie the pretty printing back to the main corporate asset, the information.

CA90s User Interface and Visualization Services provide comprehensive Reporting Services that fully exploit the new environments and technologies while protecting clients' investments (including the training investment) in existing systems. The Reporting Services provide a common solution that supports database management systems from CA and third parties across multiple platforms including IBM and similar mainframe systems, Digital VAX systems, UNIX systems, PCs under DOS and OS/2, and other environments.

The new generation reporting and printing engine for CA90s, named CA-RET for Report Engine Technology, is based on this distributed architecture. Reports are defined with a report editor on a desktop workstation. Reports may be executed directly from the desktop workstation under interactive control. The reporting engine is also available as a service to applications built with traditional programming languages, 4GLs, macro languages and nonprocedural systems, including C and C++, COBOL, CA-Visual Objects, CA-Clipper, CA-dBFast and CA-REALIZER.

The reporting engine provides powerful processing and flexible formatting including:

- Full support for different type faces, styles and sizes, as well as paragraph justification, decorative rules (lines) and other typographical elements
- Embedded graphics, useful as logos or other symbols, for example
- Columnar reporting with control-break processing, multiline detail lines, etc.
- Multicolumn "mailing label" type reports with built-in formatting for standard label sheets
- Free-form reports laid out entirely under end-user control
- Extensive calculation capabilities, including string manipulation, date processing, translation and table lookup, conditional processing and group-level processing such as percent-of-total
- Form letters with word processing capabilities such as word wrap and paragraph formatting with embedded database or calculated fields
- Sorting, filtering, translation and grouping of data
- Automatic multi-pass processing when required, for functions such as percent-of-total or summarizations in group headers

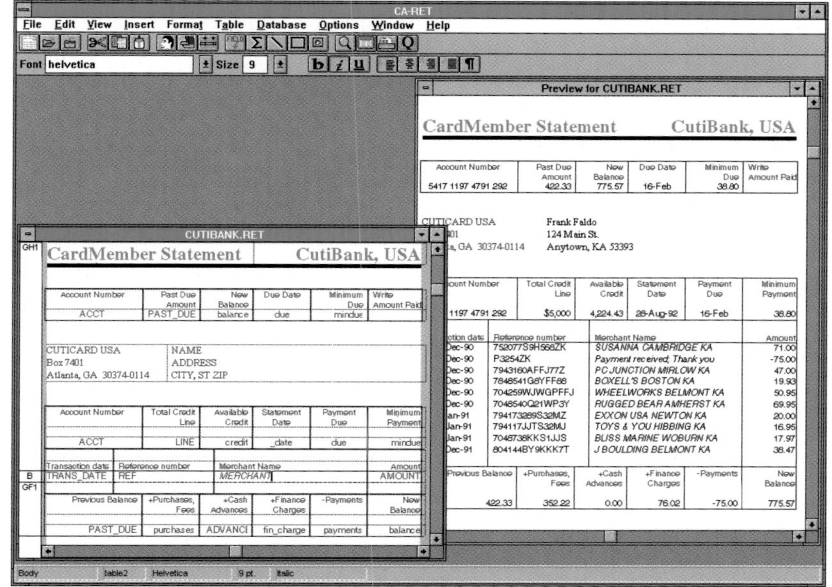

A graphical workstation combined with a laser printer is the strongest configuration for designing and producing reports that meet today's expectations on appearance. Links to databases, whether on LAN servers, midrange systems or mainframes, provide access to the main asset, corporate information. After interactive design on the GUI workstation, the system can run unattended for production reporting, with the reporting engine invoked from an application.

Defining Reports

The CA-RET reporting system provides a graphical user interface for defining the layout, formatting and data processing of reports. Based on the well-understood word processor paradigm, this WYSIWYG (What-You-See-Is-What-You-Get) interface reduces the complexity of dealing with the typographical elements. Immediate on-screen preview based on test execution with real data ensures that the layout handles the information correctly, even with such complex layouts as in-column word wrap.

The report definition includes the database query which is based on relational processing under SQL. For non-relational databases, a subset of SQL is used. A visual point-and-click user interface simplifies the creation of straightforward queries, and Query-By-Example or SQL may be used for more complex queries. This allows the more experienced user to set up a complex query, define it as a view, and let the end user directly retrieve the data.

Both the query and the report layout may be specified with variable parameters, allowing both data filters and report text to be specified at runtime.

Distributed Reporting

During execution of a report, the reporting engine retrieves data residing on the local workstation, on a database server in the LAN or on a remote midrange or mainframe system. Based on relational database access, it can combine data from multiple tables and execute queries as complex as the database engine can support.

Selecting Data

The database and file access technologies used for data collection are part of the Integration Services layer of CA90s. The data selection facility provides direct access to CA database management systems on each platform, including CA-DATACOM and CA-IDMS on mainframe, VAX, UNIX, LAN server and PC systems, CA-DB on VAX and UNIX systems and CA-Clipper, CA-dBFast and CA-Visual Objects on PC and LAN systems.

The open architecture of CA90s services provides the reporting system with access to the major third-party databases in each environment including IBM DB2 on MVS, IBM SQL/DS on VSE and VM, Digital Rdb on VAX, Oracle on VAX and UNIX systems, and various PC databases such as Microsoft SQLServer, IBM OS/2 EE Data Manager and dBASE III and IV.

Applications can invoke report execution through an API that provides for printing of the report and on-screen viewing. The reporting services can run asynchronously in the background, and the API provides queuing of report requests. The application can use the query built into the report definition, customize it with runtime parameters, or replace the query altogether. The API will also provide for direct data feed, allowing an application to report on data collected through its own methods even if it is not available in a database.

Although database management systems provide extensive processing capabilities, it is often more efficient to provide post-database sorting, translation and filtering when multiple reports are to be created from one database retrieval, each report presenting the same data from a different perspective. Processing functions such as these are necessary with simpler data sources such as VSAM, RMS and DBF.

In many cases, especially for business printouts more complex than columnar reports, the data may not be structured correctly to facilitate sophisticated printing: extensive procedural processing of the data is often required. Traditional report generators as well as conventional programming languages provide the processing capabilities to meet these more complex needs, and enterprises often have large investments in report "applications" and in the expertise to use them. For reports such as these, the procedural processing systems may be used to process the data as a front-end to the layout and formatting capabilities of the Reporting Services.

Database Query And CA-QbyX

While CA-RET directly supports database query, many applications require quite complex queries that go beyond the capabilities of the built-in, forms-based query facility of CA-RET. The Windows-based query system, CA-QbyX, provides a query-by-example facility that allows the generation of more complex queries. It may be integrated with CA-RET and with other applications. In particular, an experienced developer can use CA-QbyX to create and test-execute a complex query, perhaps with nested, correlated subqueries and other sophisticated SQL variations, and store this query as a view. End users and other developers can use this view without getting involved in the complications of its definition.

Graphics Integration

As applications increasingly support graphics, with images stored in databases, the reporting system must be able to print such pictures with the report, whether they are drawings, black-and-white scanned documents or photographs. The reporting system will draw on the image processing services of CA90s to provide these functions integrated with the report. The reporting system also provides for charting of numeric data using the CA90s charting services.

Development System Interface

A report, previously defined through the development system, may be executed independently through the standalone report generation runtime system. For integration in applications, the development systems provide interfaces to the reporting system, both standard procedural APIs and an object-oriented interface.

Both of these interfaces support runtime definition of report parameters: the query may be parameterized, for example to define the department or product covered by the report, and fixed text in the report itself may be parameterized, allowing the application to define headers and other annotation without having to redefine the report.

Both interfaces also support the execution of a report as an independent process. The application can start up a report job, perhaps queuing several jobs, and continue about its business while the report is being processed in the background.

Mainframe Reporting

These graphical workstation tools are complemented by industrial-strength report generators for heavy-duty production reporting on mainframe and midrange systems such as CA-EARL, CA-RAMIS and CA-EASYTRIEVE. These systems are language-based and will remain so in order to protect the investment clients have in often highly complex reporting programs. These procedural reporting languages are capable of far more complex processing than the nonprocedural, relational GUI reporting systems. They are able to navigate the complex data structures often used in traditional applications.

Through integration with the server versions of these systems, typographical quality reporting and workstation applications can access data collected by complex reporting programs. For example, CA-EASYTRIEVE/Server on a GUI workstation can invoke a CA-EASYTRIEVE program on a mainframe, download the results and transfer them to CA-RET, CA-dBFast, CA-Visual Objects or other systems. The data can also be transferred to CA-EASYTRIEVE/Workstation on the PC for local processing with full language compatibility.

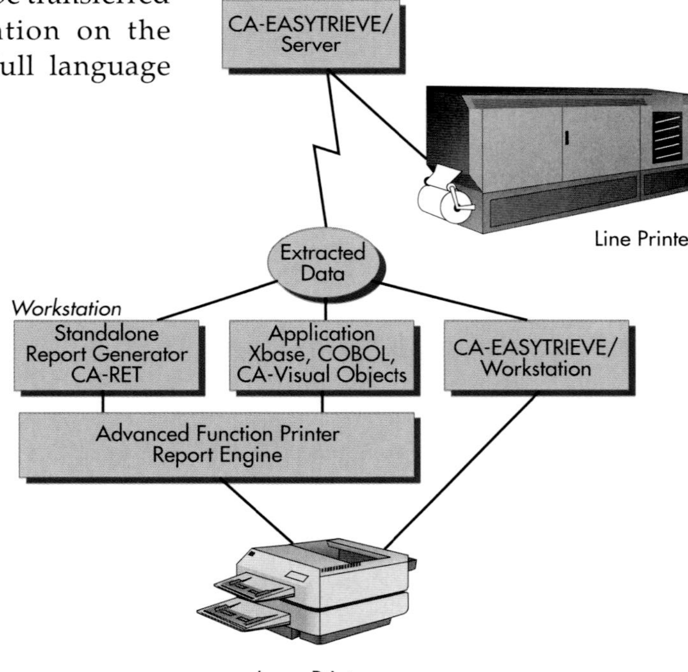

Procedural mainframe reporting systems can produce large reports with complex data processing requirements. The reporting language is also available as a server which may be invoked from a GUI utility and can feed data files to workstation tools.

APPENDIX A

Glossary Of Terms

Abstraction—The decomposition of a problem into its component levels. The most abstract level describes the components in their most general sense. *See also* Object Orientation.

Advanced Function Printing—Technology utilized by high-quality printers such as laser printers that produce near-typeset image quality output, supporting multiple typefaces, type sizes and type styles, proportionally spaced fonts, line drawings, shadings, graphics, etc. *See also* Reporting Services.

Application Development Software—The segment of Enterprise Software Solutions that provides advanced application development tools and techniques for building new, modern applications and for maintaining and enhancing existing applications. The software addresses all aspects of the application life cycle including analysis, requirements specification and planning, construction, maintenance, quality assurance and testing, and life cycle management. *See also* Enterprise Software Solutions.

Application Generator—An application development system that generates code and other application component implementations from high-level specifications. Application generators improve development productivity by exploiting the common characteristics among typical applications.

Application Programming Interface (API)—A well-defined set of function and call protocols that enable the invocation of a service from a program. The components of the CA90s Service Layers provide APIs. *See also* CA90s and Service layers.

Architecture—A blueprint for software development that usually offers a standard set of services or common functions that can be invoked through a standard set of interfaces. *See also* CA90s.

Binding—The association of code with data. Compilers typically use "early binding," the association of type-specific code with data items during the compilation step. Interpreters typically use "late binding," the deferral of this association to runtime. Systems that exhibit polymorphism, such as systems with untyped variables and object-oriented systems, exploit late binding. Early binding generally offers performance advantages and allows compile-time detection of errors, while late binding offers convenience and flexibility. A hybrid system that supports both early and late binding offers the best of both worlds.

Breakpoint—A location in a program where processing is halted during debugging. Unconditional breakpoints always halt processing; conditional breakpoints halt at the specific location if some condition is true, for example, if some variable is negative. The specification can be complex, for example halting only after 20 occurrences of the condition. A "variable watch" consists of the condition only, without any specific location.

Browsers—Components of an object-oriented development environment that facilitates code reuse by providing tools for searching based on names, contents and different kinds of relationships such as class inheritance. *See also* Integrated Development Environment.

CA90s: Computing Architecture For The 90s—Computer Associates blueprint for a software architecture and its underlying guiding principles that provide an effective, comprehensive strategy for software development that meets the needs of the Information Systems community. *See also* Guiding Principles, Service Layers, Enterprise Software Solutions and Platforms.

CAICCI—*See* Common Communication Interface.

CAICRI—*See* Common Repository Interface.

CAISQI—*See* Standard SQL Interface Services.

CASE—*See* Computer Aided Software Engineering.

Class—A definition of a set of similar objects that have the same attributes (data elements, member variables, instance variables) and the same behavior (procedures, methods, member functions). *See also* Class Library, Object and Object Orientation.

Class Library—A set of predefined classes that may be used with an object-oriented application development system. A class library is a flexible delivery vehicle for solutions and services that promotes code reuse. *See also* Application Development Software and Object Orientation.

Client/Server Architecture—Distributed application architecture in which one component, the client or requestor, requests services from another component, the server. The request may be for database services (for example, a common database server), user interface services (the architecture of the X Windows System) or application-level services (Remote Procedure Call, RPC). Client/server differs from other distribution architectures in that there is no peer-to-peer relationship. Client/server architectures are supported by the Distributed Processing Services of CA90s.

Code Generator—A component of visual development systems and application generators that generates code, typically in COBOL, C or Xbase, based on high-level specifications.

Common Communication Interface (CAICCI)—A single, consistent interface that allows communication between Enterprise Software Solutions while insulating the solutions from the specific communications and network protocol requirements within and across the operating systems and hardware platforms. The CA Common Communication Interface supports the various forms of cooperative and distributed information processing. *See also* Distributed Processing Services.

Common Repository Interface (CAICRI)—A full-function interface to CA Repository Services that allows CA software and user programs to populate, navigate and maintain information easily and consistently under the control of the repository. *See also* Repository Services and Integration Services.

Common User Access (CUA)—IBM's standard for user interfacing on designated SAA (Systems Application Architecture) platforms that is endorsed and extended to non-SAA platforms by CA90s. *See also* User Interface and Visualization Services.

Computer Aided Software Engineering (CASE)—The automation of software development, including front-end CASE tools ("upper CASE") that automate the analysis and design processes, and back-end CASE tools ("lower CASE") that automate the generation and implementation of code. *See also* Application Development Software.

Computing Architecture For The 90s—*See* CA90s.

Configuration Management—Facilities that aid in the management of complete releases of a software application, using compatible versions of component parts such as software modules, copylib members, object modules and procedures. *See also* Life Cycle Management Software.

CUA—*See* Common User Access.

Custom Controls—High-level facilities provided by the User Interface Management Services of CA90s that combine visual presentation with special processing to produce a package of functionality. *See also* User Interface and Visualization Services.

Data Scoping—Definition of the range of a program over which a variable or data item is available. *See also* Binding.

Data Typing—Definition of a variable or data item to be of a certain type and size, for example 16-bit integer, 32-bit integer, 64-bit integer, text string, logical, etc. Some systems allow the use of untyped variables, which are considered polymorphic. *See also* Binding.

Database Management Services—Components of the Integration Services layer of CA90s that enable both CA and client-written applications to flexibly store, view and manipulate enterprise information. CA Database Management Services integrate the high-production processing capabilities of navigational technology with the flexible ad hoc query facilities of relational technology in a single database management system. *See also* Integration Services, Relational Technology and Navigational Technology.

DDE—Dynamic Data Exchange, a facility of GUI environments such as Windows and OS/2 PM that allows applications to communicate information and instructions using a standard low-level protocol; the high-level semantics of the protocol must be agreed on by the applications.

Distributed Processing Services—The service layer of CA90s that insulates Enterprise Software Solutions from network and protocol requirements, and that supports the many forms of distributed processing capabilities. *See also* Common Communication Interface.

Downsizing—The process of moving existing mainframe "legacy" applications to desktop and midrange systems in order to exploit the new computing environments. *See also* Application Development Software.

Early Binding—*See* Binding.

Encapsulation—The isolation of attributes and behaviors from surrounding layers and structure. Encapsulation is an object-oriented term; it is a form of information hiding.

Enterprise Software Solutions—The layer of CA90s that comprises an extensive array of integrated software applications that address virtually every aspect of functionality in enterprises, and that utilize the Services Layers of CA90s to enhance integration, portability and ease of use. *See also* CA90s.

Environment Support Services—The facilities that provide a uniform foundation for the User Interface Management Services by providing essential functionality that may be missing in specific environments. *See also* User Interface Management Services.

Function Points—A standard metric for expressing the size of an application regardless of the language or database used to implement it. Function points are a more robust method of sizing an application than lines of source code which can vary greatly depending on the implementation language. *See also* Project Management Software.

Graphical User Interface (GUI)—Modern user interfacing technique that utilizes the graphics technology of desktop systems and terminals to enhance the presentation of textual and numeric data, graphical information and application control. Graphical User Interfaces utilize such facilities as pull-down and pop-up menus, floating dialog boxes, icons and a mouse to provide convenience and productivity advantages to end users. *See also* User Interface and Visualization Services.

Graphics Services—Components of the User Interface and Visualization Services layer of CA90s that provide powerful, standard graphics capabilities to Enterprise Software Solutions across operating systems and hardware platforms. *See also* User Interface and Visualization Services.

Guiding Principles—The underlying tenets of CA90s that govern new product development, technology acquisition and the enhancement of Computer Associates software. *See also* CA90s.

GUIs—*See* Graphical User Interface.

Image Processing—A broad term that incorporates fax quality document storage (black and white and relatively low resolutions) and photographic quality (full range gray scale or color with a high degree of fidelity). *See also* User Interface and Visualization Services.

Inheritance—The mechanism for sharing attributes and behaviors among layers of a class hierarchy. Behaviors defined at higher (more abstract) levels of the hierarchy can be accessed or redefined at a lower (more concrete) level. *See also* Abstraction and Object Orientation.

Information Hiding—*See* Encapsulation.

Instance Variables—The data items contained within an object of a class. Also called "member variables." *See also* Object Orientation.

Instantiation—Creating an object or an instance of a class. *See also* Class and Object Orientation.

Integrated Development Environment (IDE)—An integrated framework that supports all the activities involved in application development. CA-Visual Objects has an IDE called the Visual Workbench, and CA-Realia II provides an IDE for legacy COBOL systems. *See also* Iterative Development.

Integration Services—The service layer of CA90s that supports overall integration among solutions, providing new levels of integration and automation capabilities. *See also* Database Management Services and Repository Services.

Interpretive Languages—Programming languages such as BASIC and Xbase that traditionally allow fully dynamic, undeclared, untyped, unscoped variables with late (runtime) binding of operations to data. *See also* Xbase.

Iterative Development—An approach to application development based on continual refinement of prototypes into increasingly complete and correct systems. Iterative development heavily involves end users in the functional specification and external design of the system.

Late Binding—*See* Binding.

Legacy Systems—Existing applications that provide the foundation for running businesses today. Legacy systems include not only applications on mainframes, but also those midrange and desktop systems in which enterprises have made substantial investments. *See also* Downsizing.

Library Management—Facilities for controlling the components of an application during the life cycle. Library management systems typically control access and different versions. *See also* Life Cycle Management Software.

Life Cycle Management Software—The category of Application Development Software that provides automation and integration of the many tasks required to manage the development process, such as library management, version and release management, etc. *See also* Application Development Software, Library Management, Version Management, and Release Management.

Make Facility—The capability of creating jobs for all aspects of building an application including JCL generation for compilation, preprocessing, DB2 binding and other database operations.

Maintenance—The more than 80 percent of all MIS activity that is spent on bug-fixing (corrective maintenance), adding features (perfective maintenance) and adapting applications to changes in the environment (adaptive maintenance).

Method—The object-oriented code within a class that describes the procedures that enable the processing of the data. *See also* Class and Object Orientation.

Multiple Document Interface (MDI)—A way of structuring a graphical user interface in which an application displays multiple objects in separate subwindows, all contained within the overall application window. MDI is primarily used under Windows, while OS/2 PM and Motif use other ways of presenting the equivalent relationships.

Navigational Technology—Traditional database access methods, such as hierarchical, network and inverted list, that offer superior high-volume transaction processing capabilities. Both navigational and relational technologies are available in a single database management system through CA Database Management Services. *See also* Relational Technology and Database Management Services.

Object—An entity that contains both attributes (data) and behavior (procedures). A class is a data type definition; objects are instances of a class, essentially variables of that type. *See also* Object Orientation.

Object Orientation—An application development and database technology based on defining objects, abstractions of real-world entities, which contain both data and procedures. Widely used for GUI programming, object orientation is a powerful technique for facilitating code reuse in general. Object-oriented systems are based on the four concepts of classification, encapsulation, inheritance and polymorphism.

Object-Based Systems—Those development systems that exhibit some but not all of the characteristics of a true object-oriented system.

OLE—Object Linking and Embedding, a facility of GUI environments such as Windows that allows applications such as word processors to include an object, such as a graphic, in a document while retaining the link to the original file and the application that created the embedded object. OLE is implemented as a high-level protocol on top of DDE.

OOP—Object-Oriented Programming. *See* Object Orientation.

P-Code Compiler—A type of interpreter which preprocesses the code in a kind of compilation step. P-code compilers generally have better performance than interpreters, but do not match the speed and integrity of true compilers. *See also* Binding.

Platforms—The variety of operating systems and hardware environments spanning mainframe, midrange and desktop systems on which Enterprise Software Solutions execute. Through the capabilities offered by the Service Layers, CA90s promotes distributed processing and portability of Enterprise Software Solutions across the widest range of platforms. *See also* CA90s, Enterprise Software Solutions and Service Layers.

Polymorphism—The ability of variables and objects to handle different types of information and different requests for actions. Variables without data type are considered polymorphic, in that they can store different kinds of data; an object-oriented system is polymorphic in that the same message may be sent to objects of different classes.

Project Management Software—A wide range of facilities available across multiple platforms that provide end users with consistent techniques and methodologies for forecasting, planning, optimizing and controlling resources, costs and schedules related to application development projects. *See also* Application Development Software.

Prototyping—The development of a model that displays the look-and-feel of an application to be built. The prototype may be a non-functional "mock-up" that displays only the "look," it may implement navigation and user controls to display the "feel" of the application, or it may be a functional version of an application for which enhancements are prototyped. *See also* Iterative Development and Integrated Development Environment.

Relational Technology—Database access techniques that provide extensive data access flexibility through the use of SQL. Both relational and navigational technologies are available in a single database management system through CA Database Management Services. *See also* Navigational Technology and Database Management Services.

Release Management—Facilities that control where and how users are running applications by supporting and controlling software distribution, version upgrades and machine configurations in networked environments. *See also* Life Cycle Management Software.

Replaceable Database Drivers—The technological framework for the open database architecture for Xbase-style access. It allows plugging in drivers that support several different databases, with transparent access on the application level. *See also* Xbase and Integration Services.

Reporting Services—Components of the User Interface and Visualization Services layer of CA90s that provide consistent, comprehensive, and integrated reporting capabilities for Enterprise Software Solutions, across multiple platforms. Reporting Services support sophisticated processing and advanced function printing. *See also* User Interface and Visualization Services and Advanced Function Printing.

Repository Services—A component of the Integration Services layer of CA90s that provides global data dictionary facilities for sharing information across all CA Enterprise Software Solutions and across multiple platforms. Repository Services enable enterprises to complement and be compatible with hardware vendor repositories, such as the offerings of IBM and Digital, and other emerging industry standards. *See also* Integration Services.

Service Layers—Key components of CA90s that provide shared functions and technologies for integrated Enterprise Software Solutions, and that enable the software to operate across the widest range of platforms. *See also* User Interface and Visualization Services, Integration Services, and Distributed Processing Services.

SQL—Standard Query Language. A database definition and manipulation language that offers easier end-user access to enterprise data stored in database management systems using relational technology.

Standard SQL Interface Service (CAISQI)—An API that allows programs to transparently interface to different SQL databases, insulating them from the differences among database interface protocols. CAISQI supports both CA and third-party databases. *See also* Application Programming Interface and Relational Technology.

Stepwise Refinement—*See* Iterative Development.

Subclassing—The definition of a class hierarchy by defining a class as a (more concrete) special case of some more general class. *See also* Object Orientation.

Turnover Management—Facilities that ensure that all the component parts of a system have been tested and documented, and are promoted together from one release level to the next. *See also* Life Cycle Management Software.

Unstructured Data—Information that does not fit traditional information processing including the data required for image processing, pen computing (handwriting), sound and video. *See also* User Interface and Visualization Services.

User Interface And Visualization Services—The service layer of CA90s that provides the man–machine interface and that insulates developers from the complexities of underlying technologies. *See also* User Interface Management Services.

User Interface Management Services (CAIUIMS)—Components of the User Interface and Visualization Services layer of CA90s that provide graphical as well as character-based user interfacing. *See also* User Interface and Visualization Services.

Version Management—Facilities that ensure that the various changes made to software modules during the development of applications are tracked, controlled and managed, and includes the ability to simultaneously manage several different versions of the same software module. *See also* Life Cycle Management Software.

Visual Development Tools—Application development tools such as form painters and code generators that allow the definition of both visual appearance of an application and the links between menu items, buttons and data fields, and their corresponding actions. *See also* Application Development Software.

Xbase—The industry term for those database and application development systems that have a heritage in dBASE. CA Xbase products include CA-dBFast, CA-Clipper and CA-Visual Objects for Clipper, dBASE and FoxPro.

APPENDIX B

Glossary Of CA Software

Below is a listing of CA software products that have been mentioned in this book. This list is not to be construed as a complete listing of CA products since Computer Associates has over 300 software products, too many to list here. For a complete listing of CA software, please refer to the CA Software Guide.

CA-ADS—A fourth-generation application development system for CA-IDMS that incorporates a high-level programming language with nonprocedural program and application construction including screen painting, application flow control, integrated active dictionary and security facilities.

CA-C++—A platform-independent compiler for the C++ language that very closely conforms to the original AT&T specification.

CA-CASELINK—A PC-based application development tool that automatically converts the output from leading upper-CASE tools into CA-DATACOM and CA-IDEAL design objects.

CA-CommonView Class Library—The delivery vehicle for making the CAIUIMS architecture available to application developers. CA-CommonView supports C++, both CA-C++ and major third-party compilers, as well as the CA-Visual Objects systems.

CA-Clipper—An Xbase application development system and database for DOS that provides powerful extensions to the Xbase language, object orientation and a highly efficient compiler.

CA-COBOLVISION—A workstation-based analysis, debugging and visualization system that provides a GUI-based front-end for COBOL programs operating on remote hosts or on the same workstation.

CA-CONSENSUS—A PC-based application development tool that automatically converts the output from leading upper-CASE tools into CA-TELON design objects.

CA-dBFast—An Xbase application development system and database for Windows that provides GUI-oriented extensions to the language combined with visual development tools.

CA-EASYTRIEVE—A generalized information retrieval, reporting and data management tool that simplifies programming on both the mainframe and the PC.

CA-ESTIMACS—An automated project estimation and analysis tool.

CA-EZTEST—A complete online, interactive testing and debugging facility for CICS programs.

CA-FPXpert—A facility that automates and simplifies the function point counting process.

CA-IDEAL—A fourth-generation application development system for CA-DATACOM in which a high-level language is complemented by nonprocedural panel and report management, and embedded or generated SQL can be used to access data.

CA-InterTest—A complete set of interactive, menu-driven CICS debugging and testing facilities.

CA-LIBRARIAN—A comprehensive library management facility that provides secure storage and access to source code as well as automated control features and procedures.

CA-METRICS—Automated measurement tool that allows users to define key performance measures, such as actual cost versus estimated cost, time to delivery, defect ratios, and maintenance cost ratios, for monitoring and improving performance.

CA-OPTIMIZER—COBOL optimization and debugging solution that improves system performance, programmer productivity and program reliability.

CA-PAN/LCM—Complete change and configuration management for the programmable workstation environment.

CA-PANVALET—A comprehensive library management facility that centralizes the storage of source, JCL, object code and data.

CA-PLANMACS—An automated tool that provides project managers with detailed project plans based on a work breakdown structure that enables managers to determine their project needs down to the task and activity levels.

CA-QbyX—A Windows-based database query facility that supports access to SQL databases on workstations, networks, midrange systems or hosts. CA-QbyX also supports the generation of forms-based Windows applications through its visual development tools and simple scripting language.

CA-RAMIS—An end-user reporting, data retrieval and application development tool; also available as a highly functional workstation information manager.

CA-Realia—Comprehensive, mainframe-compatible COBOL development platform for the PC. It enables users to downsize mainframe applications to produce cost-effective PC-LAN-based applications, offload mainframe COBOL, DL/I, IMS and CICS program development to PC-based programmer workstations and develop state-of-the-art PC applications.

CA-REALIZER—A BASIC application development system for Windows and PM that provides GUI-oriented extensions to the language combined with visual development tools.

CA-RET—CA Report Engine Technology, a key component of the Reporting Services of CA90s, operates as a standalone report generator and may also be invoked from applications. It provides support for Advanced Function Printing and accesses various databases on several platforms.

CA-SuperProject—A comprehensive automated project management system than enables project managers to efficiently control the actual execution of projects.

CA-TELON—Application generator with design, prototyping and generation capabilities.

CA-TELON PWS—Complete implementation of the mainframe version of CA-TELON designed to run on DOS and OS/2.

CA-TRAPS—A workstation-based quality assurance tool for mainframe applications that automates testing and provides early detection of software defects.

CA-VERIFY—A quality assurance tool that automates regression testing to ensure consistent behavior of different versions and maintenance releases.

CA-Visual Objects—A family of object-oriented application development systems and databases for GUI environments, including Windows. CA-Visual Objects provides visual development tools, a repository-based IDE and a native-mode compiler. Versions of CA-Visual Objects provide compatibility with Xbase systems such as CA-Clipper, CA-dBFast, dBASE and FoxPro, and with COBOL, CA-ADS, CA-IDEAL and CA-TELON.